SANCTIFY THEM THROUGH THY TRUTH

Sanctify Them Through Thy Truth

God's Word in Human History

Mark Sweetnam

JOHN RITCHIE LTD
CHRISTIAN PUBLICATIONS

40 Beansburn, Kilmarnock, Scotland

ISBN-13: 978 1 907731 73 0

Copyright © 2012 by John Ritchie Ltd.
40 Beansburn, Kilmarnock, Scotland

www.ritchiechristianmedia.co.uk

Typeset by John Ritchie Ltd., Kilmarnock
Printed by Bell & Bain Ltd., Glasgow

Contents

Preface

The chapters that make up this volume are, in part, the result of a series of lessons on 'how we got our Bible' given to the boys and girls of the Rathmines Gospel Hall Sunday school. I am grateful to the overseers there for their willingness to allow me to take up a fairly unusual topic, and to the children who responded to it with such enthusiasm, and who allowed me to look at a familiar subject with new eyes.

Those lessons later became the basis of a series of articles that appeared in *Truth and Tidings* throughout 2010. This was followed by a second series, called 'Sanctify them through Thy truth', which appeared throughout 2011 and 2012. These articles, which essentially told two halves of the one story, have been brought together, with some additional material, in this volume. I am grateful to Dr A.J. Higgins for his invitations to contribute to *Truth and Tidings,* and for his permission to re-use material that first appeared in print there.

A number of individuals have commented on these articles, before and after their appearance in print. I particularly appreciate the helpful comments of a number of brethren, whose input has been valuable.

The structure of this book manifestly owes a great deal to the form in which this material was originally published. Although the chapters do contribute to the telling of a single story, they are more standalone than would be the case if they had not originally been monthly articles. For the same reason, there are a few minor overlaps between the material covered in different chapters.

It has been a joy to research, to teach, and to write this

material, and to appreciate, just a little more deeply, the greatness of our God as He manifests Himself to His people. It is my prayer that this book will be used of Him in the education, edification, and encouragement of His own.

Dublin, 2012

The Holy Scriptures

1. Oh Book! infinite sweetnesse! let my heart
    Suck ev'ry letter, and a hony gain,
    Precious for any grief in any part;
To cleare the breast, to mollifie all pain.

Thou art all health, health thriving, till it make
    A full eternitie: thou art a masse
    Of strange delights, where we may wish and take.
Ladies, look here ; this is the thankfull glasse,

That mends the lookers eyes: this is the well
    That washes what it shows.   Who can indeare
    Thy praise too much? thou art heav'ns Lidger here,
Working against the states of death and hell.

    Thou art joyes handsell: heav'n lies flat in thee,
    Subject to ev'ry mounters bended knee.

2. Oh that I knew how all thy lights combine,
    And the configurations of their glorie!
    Seeing not only how each verse doth shine,
    But all the constellations of the storie.

    This verse marks that, and both do make a motion
    Unto a third, that ten leaves off doth lie:
    Then as dispersed herbs do watch a potion,
    These three make up some Christians destinie.

    Such are thy secrets, which my life makes good,
    And comments on thee: for in ev'ry thing
    Thy words do finde me out, and parallels bring,
    And in another make me understood.

    Starres are poore books, and oftentimes do misse
    This book of starres lights to eternall blisse.

George Herbert

CHAPTER 1

History and the Believer

According to Henry Ford, the renowned American carmaker, 'history is more or less bunk'. He went on to proclaim his belief that the past was irrelevant and that only the present mattered. While this mind-set has not vanished entirely, only a very few would agree with him. History fascinates us. The shelves of our bookshops and our libraries provide ample evidence that we cannot get enough of it. For some, it is the personal aspect of history that is most compelling – the lives of great men and women, their triumphs and their failings, the way in which, for better or for worse, they wielded great power. For others, it is the smooth and inscrutable operations of the political machine that most enthral, the rise and fall of party and faction, the struggle between idealism and self-interest, the loyalties and the betrayals that have helped to shape our world. And for others, the charm of history is not found on the large canvas, but in the intricate and intimate details of the everyday lives of ordinary people – men and women who are, simultaneously, so like and so unlike ourselves. But whatever it is that draws to history, we read it and study it because we believe it to be more than mere 'bunk', because we are convinced that it does have something relevant to say to our own time.

To believe that history is irrelevant 'bunk', the story of a dead past that should be buried and forgotten, is reprehensible in any context. It is a particularly incomprehensible view for the believer. As Christians, history has a special importance for us and we ought, therefore, to have a special interest in history. For we know history to be more than the effects of blind and random chance. We see, or we should see, a value in the past that goes beyond a recognition of a humanity shared with our forebears. The most cursory examination of our Bibles will confirm that we have a God to Whom history matters.

Our God is a God who has *intervened* in history. The God revealed to us in the Bible is not the remotely transcendent deity imagined by some. Though God 'inhabits Eternity' (Isa 57:15), He has created a universe bounded by time as well as space. But He did not create time and abandon it to randomness. Rather, He intervenes in it, reveals Himself in it, and, in the Incarnation of Christ, Himself entered it. The shape and texture of history come from God and reveal His wisdom and might just as surely as every other facet of His marvellous creation.

But our God is also *interested* in history. This would be a difficult conclusion to avoid even for someone encountering the Bible for the very first time. He would begin at Genesis, and find book after book devoted to historical record, to the actions and events of generation after generation of the people of God. Archaeologists and historians have wondered at the accuracy of this record, and those who study the writing of history accord Scripture a special place. They all recognise what could not very easily be denied – that history matters to God, and that He has given it a special prominence in His revelation.

Nor is this accidental. The God who intervenes and Who has so great an interest in history also *instructs* us through history. It was this great purpose of history, and the attitude that it demands from us that Paul spoke of in 1 Cor. 10:11 – 'Now all these things happened unto them for ensamples: and they are written for our admonition, upon whom the ends of the world are come.' As believers, we have an obligation to be instructed and admonished by those who have gone before, to live as those who 'are compassed about with so great a cloud of witnesses' (Heb. 12:1). This imperative means that faithful history cannot be an airbrushed picture of idyllic bliss: it must be accurate and honest. There can be a tendency, when historians describe events that distress us, to shoot the messenger, to blame the historian for the story he is telling. To do so is to misunderstand the true purpose of history. We ought not to feel any glee in recording or reading the weaknesses of others, but a quick glance at Biblical history will remind us that 'for our admonition', God has provide comprehensive and accurate accounts of the past – the good as well as the bad, the praiseworthy with the reprehensible.

For the believer, Biblical history is of the greatest interest and importance. It has been recorded for us by the inspiration of the Holy Spirit, and its accuracy and its implications are thus safeguarded for us. But, after that must surely come an interest in church history. By this, we mean not the history of any institution – whatever the institution these are likely to make depressing reading – but the history of how the people of God have sought to maintain testimony for Him throughout the centuries that have passed since the birth of the church at Pentecost. That account, too, is not without its depressing elements, but it is also a stirring and cheering story of the unchanging unwavering faithfulness of God to His people, and the faithfulness – though feeble and faltering – of His people to Him.

It is also a long story, encompassing two millennia, and a complicated one. In this volume we shall only be able to look at it in a very sketchy fashion. But even so, we can learn a great deal that is of pressing contemporary significance in our consideration. In particular, there are two outstanding lessons that we should grasp.

Firstly, we should appreciate afresh the importance of the Word of God to the people of God. As we trace the history of the church, we very soon discover that the word of God has been an indispensible source of spiritual strength and prosperity. Only when her focus and dependence has been firmly fixed on the Scriptures has she been effective in testimony for God. This is a truth that can never be too often emphasised. As believers, we need 'the whole counsel of God' (Acts 20:27).

We cannot do without it, and if these chapters make us appreciate this vital fact more clearly, they will not have been in vain.

We will also come to realise something about the power of error. The history of the church, indeed, is a history of the struggle between truth and error. This should not dismay us – Scripture makes it abundantly clear that truth will inevitably be subject to satanic attack. Furthermore, 1 Cor. 11:19 reminds us that error is not only inevitable, but that it is necessary: 'For there must be also heresies among you, that they which are approved may be made manifest among you'. And we will see that repeatedly this is what has happened – the attack of error has resulted in truth being more clearly defined and more zealously defended. It is never healthy to be too much occupied with error, but it is important to be able to recognise it. Given that the errors of the past are constantly being repackaged as the latest and most exciting doctrine, we can learn valuable lessons from history. After all, 'those who cannot remember the past are condemned to repeat it'.

We are, and we should be, fascinated by history. We can, and we should be instructed by it – inspired by its paragons and admonished by its failures. But, if we understand the fact that God's power and providence are manifested in history, our consideration of it should, and must, move us to worship His wisdom and His power. That was certainly the result of Habakkuk's contemplation of the past. In chapter 3 of his prophecy, he begins his great prayer, with its account of God's might and its ringing affirmation of His faithfulness, with words that express a true understanding of the significance of history: 'O Lord, I have heard the report of thee, and am afraid: O Lord, revive thy work in the midst of the years, in the midst of the years make it known; in wrath remember mercy.' (Hab. 3:2, R.V.). From his consideration of the past Habakkuk drew strength for the present and a renewed trust in God. May God grant that our consideration will do the same for each one of us.

CHAPTER 2

'A more sure word of prophecy'

Peter's second epistle records for us the last words written by the Apostle. Conscious that he would shortly be called upon to 'put off' his 'tabernacle' (1:14), he wrote to 'stir up' the believers (v.13) and to prepare them for the coming day when the apostolic voice would be silent, when those who had known the Lord on Earth would all have gone home to Heaven. As Peter seeks to edify his readers, he is careful to remind them that the message that he preached was not a 'cunningly devised fable' (v. 16) but, in truth, the word of God. As he outlines the credentials of his message he looks back to the 'holy mount' (v.18), and to the experiences that he had there – what he saw (v.16), and what he heard (v.18). Had Peter been a modern evangelical, he likely would have stopped there: offering the subjective and the experiential as the basis for Christian life and testimony. But he wasn't and he didn't. Rather, he makes one of the greatest claims for the importance of Scripture found anywhere in its pages when he turns away from the great experiences that he had, and points the believers who would come after him, not to the sensual but to Scripture – to the 'more sure word of prophecy' (v.19)

The basis for our Christianity has not changed in the intervening years. Though we are far removed from the days of the Apostles, and have never had the privilege of knowing them personally, we are not at a disadvantage to believers of the first century for we have, as they did, a sure word of prophecy, a revelation from God that He has designed to be reliable, dependable, and absolutely sure.

But Peter's readers might well have asked what it is that makes God's word so secure. We have a natural tendency to trust what we can verify by our senses, and when that isn't possible, we look for an eyewitness, for someone who was there. How, then, can we be expected not only to rely on Scriptures written centuries ago, but even give them greater weight than the evidences of our senses. Peter anticipates the question, and provides the answer. And the answer is inspiration.

Peter doesn't use the word inspiration here. Indeed, the word is only found once in our English New Testament, in II Tim 3:16, where it could be literally translated 'God-breathed.' But while Peter doesn't use the term, he gives a more comprehensive account of how inspiration works than any other New Testament writer:

> 'For the prophecy came not in old time by the will of man: but holy men of God spake as they were moved by the Holy Ghost.' (2 Pe. 1:21)

These are crucial details. Firstly, Peter emphasises the provenance of Scripture – it comes from God. Those used by God in the writing of Scripture did not decide, of their own volition, that they would write Scripture. The revelation of the Bible is God's revelation of His person and character and it originates with Him, and not with man.

Next, Peter tells us about the people that were used. There is a paradox here that we cannot fully understand. God was inspiring Scripture, when written down it would be the word-perfect revelation of Divine truth. But personality still matters. It matters because the writers had to be holy men. It matters too because, as we read the books of the Bible, we recognise individual vocabularies, individual styles and individual personalities at work. The inspiration of Scripture does not mean that God dictated His word to secretaries: the process was more complex than that.

Finally, Peter describes the power behind inspiration – the

human authors of Scripture were inspired, they were borne along by the Holy Ghost. This is what Paul means, in II Tim 3:16, when he speaks of Scripture as 'God-breathed'. It is ever the work of the Holy Spirit to reveal God. He was involved at Creation and the Incarnation. He is central also to the great work of inspiration, ensuring that as the Scriptures reveal God they provide us with a basis for our faith that is absolutely solid, that is 'more sure'.

There are two other important details about inspiration that do not feature in this passage. And, when we use the term inspiration it is often useful to define more carefully what we mean by that term. We believe that the Bible teaches the *plenary* and *verbal* inspiration of scripture.

Plenary inspiration simply means that 'all Scripture is given by inspiration of God' (II Tim 3:16). In other words, all of Scripture reveals God, and we need all of that revelation. Genesis 1:1 is as vital as John 3:16, but so too is Ezekiel 3:3. There is not a verse of Scripture that we can do without. We should also note that all Scripture is equally inspired. There is a trend in some circles to differentiate between the value of the directly spoken words of Christ and Paul's epistles. But this misses the truth of plenary inspiration. In truth, the epistles of Paul or of John are just as much the word of God as the Beatitudes.

The verbal inspiration of Scripture is equally important. It holds that God did not simply inspire the writers of the Bible with general ideas, and then leave them to figure out the best words with which those ideas were to be expressed. Again, II Tim 3:16 makes this clear. Paul does not say that the ideas behind Scripture were given by inspiration. He does not even say that the books of the Bible were given by inspiration. Instead, he focuses on what is written (the word translated Scripture is *graphe*, literally, writings), and as words, and not concepts are written down, it must be the very words, and not merely the ideas that they embody that God has given by inspiration. Other

17

passages too speak of Divine inspiration of words (II Sam. 23:2, *cf.* Acts 1:16; Jer. 1:9). Similarly, the Lord Jesus himself drew the attention of His enemies to individual words of Scripture. In Mt 22:41-46 and Jn 10:34-36, He bases His argument on the individual words of Old Testament Scripture. So too does the Apostle Paul, in Gal. 3:16, where the difference between a singular and a plural, a difference of letters, rather than words, is shown to be the result of Divine design and inspiration.

In Matt. 5:18, the Lord Jesus promised 'one jot or one tittle shall in no wise pass from the law, till all be fulfilled.' In speaking these words, He was making a clear claim for the certainty of Scripture. But He was also making a claim for its accuracy, right down to the dots on the i's and the crosses on the t's. God does not want us to be unsure of our ground, to be uncertain in our understanding of His person and ways. In His infinite and sovereign wisdom He has provided us with the Scriptures. And, in order that we might rely entirely upon them, He has given them by means of plenary verbal inspiration, and we can rest on the 'more sure word of prophecy'.

CHAPTER 3

From Moses to me – Divine sovereignty and the preservation of Scripture

God has revealed Himself to us in Scripture. That revelation was given to holy men by means of inspiration, a process that was initiated, empowered, and overseen by God Himself. But, seeing that this took place up to four thousand years ago, it is clear that the revelation inspired by God had to be preserved through the centuries. The story of its preservation seems, at times, an astoundingly human one. It involves priests, preachers, and politicians. Some of the characters in the story had motives that were holy and pure, others moved in response to the promptings of ego, personal relationships, or political expediency. Yet, for all the messy humanity of the narrative, those with eyes to see it can find clear traces of the sovereign hand of God, moving providentially to ensure the preservation and transmission of Scripture from the time of Moses down to the present day.

God's providential preservation of Scripture has not always taken the course that we, with human wisdom, might have expected. For example, none of the *autographs* of Scripture survive. Autographs are the original texts, written by the prophets, the apostles, or their amanuenses. So, we cannot point to a manuscript in the hand of Paul or of John in any of the libraries or museums of the world. To us, this does seem strange. Why would God have His people rely on copies, when He could have seen to it that the originals were preserved? It is not for us to question the way in which God has worked, or to attempt to second guess His motives. His way, after all, is perfect. But there are two possible reasons for His acting in this way. Firstly, God's people in every age have had the tendency to erect idols, and to give to material objects the worship that is due to God alone. One can hardly begin to imagine the industry of idolatry that would have built up around any surviving autograph of Scripture. Secondly, right from its infancy, the Church has been attacked by heresies. Scripture in the hands of God's people has always been the weapon with which these heresies have been met. But suppose one organisation or individual were able to claim that they, alone, had access to the authoritative version of scripture. Even without surviving autographs, this is not unprecedented in Christian history. God, by ensuring the transmission of Scripture in many copies has made it impossible for any one to claim a monopoly on Divine truth.

So Scripture was not preserved in its original manuscripts. But it was preserved in the multitude of *apographs* or copies that were made. Reverent scribes, both Jewish and Christian, painstakingly and accurately copied out the Scriptures. Because they all held the truth of the plenary and verbal inspiration of Scripture, they would take the utmost care in their copying. Both those who supervised their work and the end users of the text would, likewise, carefully ensure the accuracy and reliability of the copy. Mistakes would be made: the scribes were human. But the differences introduced by these mistakes would be minor and would in no way undermine any Biblical doctrine.

These copies were written on two different media. In II Tim. 4:13, the apostle Paul mentions 'books and parchments' that he wishes to have with him in jail. We don't know what the contents of those books and parchments were, but these two forms of written text had been the media for the transmission of Scripture right from the start.

Parchment is made from animal skin, usually the hide of a sheep or goat. Dried and scraped free of its hair it made a smooth writing surface. For ease of use, stitched together parchments were rolled into scrolls. It was a scroll of this sort that Jehudi cut with his penknife (Jer. 36), and that the Lord Jesus read from in the synagogue in Nazareth (Luke 4:17-20). These scrolls were very durable, but they were also expensive and bulky.

For these reasons, many of the books of the New Testament were transmitted in a new form. Technically known as the *codex* (plural *codices*), these books were formed from pages of papyrus. These thin sheets were made by laying rows of reeds in alternating directions and beating them flat. Unlike parchments, these papyrus codices were cheap and easily transportable. The latter virtue was particularly appealing to the persecuted Christians of the first century who required books that could readily be concealed and easily carried. However, papyrus is far less durable than parchment, and is especially susceptible to damage by damp. It is for this reason that most of the papyri that have survived have been found in hot and dry desert climates.

In these forms, thousands of portions of Scripture survive. There are more testimonies to the text of Scripture than there are to any other text of similar age. In fact scholars who work on more recent texts, right up to the sixteenth and seventeenth centuries, frequently have to make do with far fewer witnesses to textual accuracy. Rather than allowing any monopoly on the text of Scripture, God has spread it widely.

When the texts of these manuscript portions are compared, some inconsistencies or disagreements emerge. This gives rise to the work of textual scholars who pore over different manuscript readings, attempting to determine what reading is the best attested and most accurate. Their work is important. Sometimes, however, when we read works of textual criticism, the focus is so much on the differences that we lose sight of the vast amount of agreement that there is between all these manuscripts, written across the centuries, and found scattered all over the Middle East. Those who oppose the claims of Scripture like to cite vast numbers of 'inconsistencies', but seldom outline how minor the disagreements are – often at the level of variations in spelling. These blips that have been introduced as the text of Scripture was transmitted through the centuries in no way imperil the truth of the Bible. Even the most radical critical editions of the Biblical text teach all the doctrines of Christianity.

God has given us His word. And, having given that word, He has seen to it that it would be preserved to reveal His person and His ways long after those to whom it was first given had been taken to Heaven. In His sovereignty, He has overruled so that believers in this twenty-first century do not need to grope after Divine truth, or to reconstruct it from a few scattered fragments. He has given us a Book unlike any other, and in confidence and with safety we can receive and obey it.

CHAPTER 4

The End of the Apostolic Era

Some time in the year 62 AD, an oddly assorted group of men gathered at the town of Miletus, on the shores of the Aegean Sea. They had travelled the 50 miles from nearby Ephesus at the summons of the man who now stood in their midst. He was not a physically impressive figure – short, bow-legged, and scarred from much mistreatment. For all that, the men listened hungrily to his words. This man, after all, was Paul, the apostle who had endured so much hardship that the gospel might reach them, who had been instrumental in their salvation, and who had instructed them in the truth of God. Now, as he summarised his ministry to them, they nodded in agreement, the memories of his faithfulness from the first day flooding back.

But as they listened to Pauls' words, the reminiscent smiles faded, their faces displayed disbelief and then, with welling tears, deep grief. Their beloved guide and mentor was telling them, with a clarity that left no room for misunderstanding, that they would see his face no more. For all their bluntness, the words seemed incomprehensible. How could it be that the apostle was going to be taken from them? How would they, how would the other churches survive without his support and guidance?

The apostle understood how they were feeling, and had the answer to the questions that burgeoned in their minds. Reminding them that he had declared to them 'all the counsel of God' (Acts 20:27), he directed them to the on-going source of their preservation and guidance: 'And now, brethren, I commend you to God, and to the word of His grace, which is able to build you up, and to give you an inheritance among all them which are sanctified' (v. 32). The full implications of this great commendation may not have immediately penetrated the grief of the Ephesian elders but, in days that lay ahead, they would surely have begun to understand the value of the resources to which Paul had directed them. True, the apostle was gone and they could no longer hear his voice or seek his advice. But they had assets of even greater value than the apostle. They had the same God, and they had 'the word of His grace', and that was sufficient to edify and to preserve both them and their flock.

There is a great poignancy and tenderness about the event recorded in Acts 20. But it can hardly have been unique. Many churches must have experienced a similar grief and sense of loss as the apostolic era began to draw to an end. And such believers must surely have turned with renewed eagerness to the word of God as their most vital support and guide. It is certainly significant that the three apostolic writers of Scripture each emphasise the importance and the value of Scripture in their final writings.

We can see this very clearly in Peter's second epistle. Like Paul, he is careful to warn those to whom he writes of his approaching departure: 'Knowing that shortly I must put off this my tabernacle, even as our Lord Jesus Christ hath shewed me' (II Pe. 1:14). And for Peter, too, it was a foremost priority that those who had benefitted from his ministry would be 'able after [his] decease to have these things always in remembrance' (v.15). So he reminds them once again of the reality and the certainty of the 'power and coming of Jesus Christ' (v.16). He attests to the authenticity of these events, based on what he saw (v.16) and what he heard (v.18). But this assurance might well have served to deepen the gloom of his readers. After all, they had in Peter a wonderful link with the events of the Incarnation. But he himself had warned them that that link was about to break. Could anything possibly take the place of the apostle and his experiential knowledge of Christ? Peter's answer is yes. In fact, the resource to which he points them supersedes and surpasses even his first-hand testimony: 'We have also a more sure word of prophecy; whereunto ye do well that ye take heed, as unto a light that shineth in a dark place, until the day dawn, and the day star arise in your hearts' (v.19). For Peter, it is the *certainty* of Scripture that stands out. The believers would soon be without any surviving witnesses of Christ's life and death, but they would not be in any real sense impoverished. They had the record of the apostles, and they had a more sure word of prophecy. Neither they nor we have been left at a disadvantage – Scripture, inspired by the Holy Spirit, has a reliability beyond the impressions of our senses.

We have already seen Paul's concern that the Ephesian elders be directed, in his absence, to the Word of God. In his final writing he displays precisely the same concern. As part of his final charge to Timothy, Paul reminds him of the value and reliability of Scripture 'given by inspiration of God' (II Tim. 3:16). He also stresses the *comprehensiveness* and sufficiency of Scripture – it is 'profitable for doctrine, for reproof, for correction, for instruction in righteousness: that the man of God may be perfect, throughly furnished unto all good works' (II Tim 3:16-17). No possible spiritual need of God's people goes unaddressed by the Bible – in it there is provision for every exigency of the Christian life. No other formation was required – no additional education or training was necessary for Timothy's preparation to 'every good work', and none is necessary for ours. It is noteworthy that it is Peter, the apostle who had so much first-hand experience of Christ, who prefers revelation above experience. The learned Paul, who had an education that Peter – or we – could only dream of, emphasises that Scripture, and Scripture alone is comprehensively sufficient to ensure that 'the man of God might be 'throughly furnished unto all good works'

John, too, has important truth about Scripture to impart. The book of Revelation brings to a close not only his writings, but Scripture itself. As John prepares to lay down his pen at the close of the book, he stresses not so much the certainty or the comprehensiveness of Scripture but its *completeness*: 'For I testify unto every man that heareth the words of the prophecy of this book, If any man shall add unto these things, God shall add unto him the plagues that are written in this book: and if any man shall take away from the words of the book of this prophecy, God shall take away his part out of the book of life, and out of the holy city, and from the things which are written in this book' (Rev. 22:18-19). In the context, John is speaking particularly about the book of Revelation. However, his words apply with equal force to Scripture as a whole. God's revelation cannot be added to or taken from. It cannot be added to for we have all that we need. It cannot be taken from for we need all that we have. In Scripture, God has provided a complete guide for His church. We have 'the whole counsel of God' and nothing more or less than that could be sufficient to direct His people through the centuries of testimony.

The vast majority of the Church's history took place after the departure of the apostles. Yet, it is not a history of an impoverished Church left to grope her way in a vague and uncertain twilight. God's people had – and have – God's word and, so long as they heed and obey that revelation, so long will they prosper in testimony. Far from being impoverished, we have in the completed canon of Scripture a spiritual wealth of certainty, comprehensiveness, and completeness.

CHAPTER 5

'Into all the world' – Divine Providence and the availability of the Scriptures

It is the will of God that the gospel should be preached all over the globe. When the Lord Jesus spoke to His disciples immediately before His resurrection, He outlined a service and a message with an international scope: 'ye shall be witnesses unto me both in Jerusalem, and in all Judaea, and in Samaria, and unto the uttermost part of the earth' (Acts 1:8). The book of the Acts records the obedience of the apostles to Christ's command, charting the spread of the gospel throughout the world as it was known in that day.

The apostles faced many formidable obstacles to their evangelical work. Natural, human, and infernal powers hindered their movement and endangered their lives. The propagation of the gospel was often purchased at a costly price. But one obstacle to their efforts is notable by its absence from the Scriptural record. Though many missionaries of our own day identify the challenge of the language barrier among their most formidable difficulties, the Acts does not suggest that difficulties in communication often stood in the apostles' way. This is not because they had the gift of tongues. Scripture makes it clear that the focus of that spectacular and short-lived gift was testimony to Israel, and we seek in vain for any indication that tongues assisted missionary outreach to Gentiles. Rather, in a remarkable movement of Divine providence, God had prepared the way of His servants, and had demolished the language barriers that would otherwise have slowed the spread of the gospel.

That preparation had begun seven and a half centuries before the birth of Christ as the expansion of Greek colonisation began to diffuse Greek culture and language throughout the European world. This process continued until the waning power of the Persian Empire was finally crushed, and the Greek Empire, the kingdom of brass foretold by Daniel, emerged in conquest (Daniel 2:39). At the head of this empire stood Alexander the Great, the brilliant military strategist who wept because there were no more worlds to conquer. His Empire did not long survive his death in 323 B.C., but its impact on the culture of the then known world was profound. Alexander's policy of Hellenization diffused Greek culture beyond the political boundaries of his Empire and, with that culture, came the Greek language. Thus it is that the Lord, Himself, spoke Greek, and thus it is that His apostles could move throughout the world unhindered by linguistic barriers in the spread of the gospel. And, when they came to write the gospels and the epistles, the fact that they wrote in the *koine* Greek commonly spoken by all peoples of the Roman Empire made the New Testament universally accessible.

That happened centuries later. Alexander's empire had an even greater part to play in the purposes of God. Alexandria, the city which he founded as his imperial capital, was not just a centre of political power. It was also an important cultural and educational centre. Its library, in particular, was the wonder of the ancient world, and was intended not just to house the best of Greek learning, but to gather important documents from around the world. Among these documents was the Hebrew Bible, the collection of books that we recognise as the Old Testament. And, in keeping with the aims of Alexandria's great library, it is here that the Old Testament Scriptures were first translated into Greek.

This Greek translation of the Old Testament is known as the Septuagint or LXX (seventy in Roman numerals). Both these titles refer to the tradition that the work of translation was carried out in seventy-two days by seventy – or seventy-two –

rabbis. In fact, the translation is likely to have taken a longer time than this legend would indicate – scholars suggest that, while the translation of the Pentateuch began in the third century before Christ, the translation was most probably not completed for nearly a hundred years. The significance of the Septuagint was enormous. It became the Bible of the Greek speaking Hellenistic Jewish diaspora, used throughout the classical world. It brought the knowledge of the One True God to those lost in the darkness of polytheistic Greek religion. And it provided the Lord Jesus, the disciples, and the early Christians with their Old Testament.

In a very remarkable way, God overruled the fate of nations, their armies, and their culture that the world might be prepared to receive the good news concerning the death and resurrection of His Son. But He did not merely smooth the way for the apostles and evangelists to communicate their message. He saw to it that the written Word of God, the Scriptures that lent authority and certainty to the messages preached by the apostles, would also be available to every creature in every nation.

The story of the Septuagint has an even wider significance for the study in hand in this book. Its use by the Lord Jesus and His disciples does not indicate the wholesale endorsement of what was a somewhat patchy translation. But it does give Divine approval to the principle of translating the Scriptures. God intended His word to be accessible, and He saw to it that the New Testament was not inspired in the elegant but inaccessible Greek of the classical age. Rather, Scripture was written down in the *koine* Greek spoken by the common people, in a straightforward and unadorned idiom.

It was something of this truth that Paul expressed as he stood in the Areopagus in Athens, the epicentre of Hellenistic learning and culture. Addressing the renowned philosophers of that great city he pointed them to a God whom they described as unknown:

'God that made the world and all things therein ... hath made of one blood all nations of men for to dwell on all the face of the earth, and hath determined the times before appointed, and the bounds of their habitation; That they should seek the Lord, if haply they might feel after him, and find him, though he be not far from every one of us: For in him we live, and move, and have our being.'

There could, perhaps, be no better commentary on the way in which a sovereign and provident God determined the times and the bounds of nations to ensure that the gospel message, and the Word of God that embodied it would come, with an equal lack of linguistic barrier, 'to the Jew first, and also to the Greek' (Rom. 1:16).

CHAPTER 6

Identifying Scripture:
Clarifying the Canon

The Bible is the word of God, given by inspiration of the Holy Spirit, and preserved by Divine providence. Though written millennia ago, it remains relevant and important for the twenty-first century. As such, it should not surprise us that Scripture has repeatedly been the object of satanic attack. For centuries, the enemies of the truth of Scripture have done their best to suppress it. Since the eighteenth century, the emphasis of their opposition has shifted: its object no longer to suppress Scripture, but to discredit it. First, Scripture came under attack from higher critics in the universities. Under their assault, Scripture endured: the attackers have exhausted themselves but the truth of God has remained impervious. In recent years the attack has shifted again. What genuine scholarship has been unable to achieve is now being attempted by the uninformed but imaginative efforts of novelists and filmmakers. They have suggested that Scripture is the result, not of Divine inspiration and preservation but of a grubby but successful conspiracy by powerful and power-hungry elements within the Roman Catholic Church. Their allegations are fiction, impure and simple, but they possess an extraordinary power to convince the man and woman on the street. And in no area is this imagined conspiracy more powerful than in relation to the canon of Scripture.

The word canon comes from the Greek term for a measuring line or rod. In the context of Scripture, we use the term to refer to the list of books that we recognize as the Bible, the authoritative word of God. It is easy, perhaps, to take the sixty six books of our Bible for granted, but we must remember that each of these books originally circulated on its own and that it is only after the time of the apostles that the Bible, as we know it, appeared.

The Old Testament canon was not a difficult question – Christianity had inherited those books that the Jews had, for centuries, recognized and revered as the oracles of God (Rom. 3:2). A handful of books found in the Greek Septuagint but not in the Hebrew Old Testament were accepted by some, but were generally recognized as lying outside the canon. But the question was more complicated in relation to the New Testament canon. In addition to the books of the New Testament, there were other books purporting to tell the story of the life of Christ, and other letters purporting to come from the apostles. It is important to recognise that decisions did have to be taken as to which books had the authority of God's word, and which did not. The process of taking these decisions took some time, and often it was driven by the need to reply to the attempts of heretics to impose their own ideas about the content of the canon on the church.

The fact that such decisions had to be made and had to be made by men, has been highlighted recently in popular culture and in the media. The suggestion seems to be that the canon of Scripture was cooked up by a powerful cartel of clergy who got together, and eliminated from the canon books that did not agree with their preconceived ideology.

But this is far from the reality of the situation. The church councils that settled the issue of the canon were not creating the Bible from scratch, starting with a blank sheet and literally making it up as they went along. Rather, they were ratifying, or giving their seal of approval, to books that Christians had long recognized as Scripture. It is for this reason that, in spite of suggestions that the canon as it now exists was simply the option endorsed by the group that shouted loudest, there was a consensus on most of the canon, and real debate about only a handful of books.

Thus, one of the earliest lists of the New Testament books, from Tertullian in 150 AD contains most of the books that make up our New Testament today. A later list, called the 'Muratorian Fragment', and dating from between 170 and 210 accepts most of the books in our Bible but rejects Hebrews, James, I and II Peter and III John. The first surviving list containing just the twenty seven books found in our New Testament was written by Athanasius of Alexandria (*c*.293-373) around 367. That list of twenty seven books was recognised by the professing church of the day in the Council of Carthage in 397, and that recognition largely silenced the debate about the canon. Again, it was not the decision of this Council that made these books Scripture. Rather, the Council of Carthage codified the list of books that the majority of Christians everywhere had recognized as Scripture all along.

We need therefore to have no doubt about the authority of any of the books that we find between the covers of our Bibles. They take their place there not because of a conspiracy but because they have had, for believers of all ages, the authority and power unique to the Word of God. Equally, when the covers of our magazines and the pages of our newspapers trumpet the discovery of a 'new gospel' whose contents challenge the truth of Scripture, we need not be alarmed or shaken. There is nothing new about this. The apostle Paul found it necessary to warn the Thessalonians 'that ye be not soon shaken in mind, or be troubled, neither by spirit, nor by word, nor by letter as from us, as that the day of Christ is at hand' (II Thess 2:2). The Gnostic heresy that was the object of Paul's most direct and forceful rebuttal produced spurious gospels and epistles then, and these documents and their teachings have enjoyed a new popularity in our day. We are assailed by many efforts to insert false and heretical books into the canon of Scripture. In the face of this onslaught, we, like the Thessalonians, have no need to be shaken or troubled, we can rely with certainty on our Bibles knowing that there, and there alone we find the unique and authoritative word of God.

CHAPTER 7

Marcion and the Attack on the Canon

The Word of God is vital to the health of His Church. Only by it can she be instructed, directed, and safely guarded through a hostile world. It is, therefore, hardly surprising that very early in her history she faced a serious attack on Scripture. On the results of this conflict much depended. Would the people of God be left with a mutilated Bible, arrogantly trimmed to suit the fancies of one man or a group of men? Or would they go on in testimony garrisoned and guided by the whole counsel of God, Scripture in all its wealth and fulness?

The attack came in the teachings of Marcion of Sinope. Marcion came from Pontus, a Roman province in what is now Turkey. Around the year 140, he came to Rome where he began to spread a novel – and heretical – teaching that attacked both the Church and Scripture. In doing so, he developed tendencies that had already been at work during the lifetime of the apostles and which had been addressed in the epistles.

One of these tendencies was Gnosticism. This belief system was a syncretism between Greek philosophy and Christianity and is addressed, particularly, by the epistles to the Galatians and to the Colossians. The most important teaching of the Gnostics was that matter was inherently evil. As a consequence, they denied the truth of the incarnation, arguing, instead, that the physical body of the Lord Jesus was an illusion and that he remained at all times an incorporeal spirit (a view known as Docetism). Marcion added a new twist to this teaching, arguing that the Bible spoke of two Gods: the God of the Jews who had created matter and the God of the New Testament who was utterly transcendent, loving, and compassionate. This view had major implications for Marcion's view of Judaism, the Old Testament, and the Gospels.

As the Acts of the Apostles and the epistles make clear, tensions between saved Jews and Gentiles within the church were nothing new – they had been a recurring problem throughout the first century. Now, in Marcion's teachings, this tension rose, once more, to the surface.

Marcion has been described as a 'theological anti-Semite'. And that anti-Semitism was most clearly seen in his view of Scripture. As the Old Testament spoke of a Jewish God, Marcion entirely repudiated its authority for and relevance to the Christian church. Nor did he stop there. He recognised that much of the New Testament was based firmly on Old Testament Scripture, and set about purifying Scripture of this inheritance. He thought very highly of the writings of Paul, but rejected the authority of the other apostles because, as he saw it, their Christianity was corrupted by their Jewish background and inclination. Moreover, the gospels were also not to be trusted. They had been tampered with by Judaizers intent on distorting the life and the message of Christ.

In the light of this there was nothing to be done but to produce a 'purified' version of Scripture. This Marcion did. He produced a canon of his own. This consisted of two parts. The first was 'The Gospel', a 'de-judaized' version of the gospel of Luke. The second was called 'The Apostle', and comprised a cleaned up version of the first ten Pauline epistles.

Marcion's arrogance was staggering. On no authority but his own, he had launched a full-scale attack on the text of Scripture. Only what he deemed suitable could be allowed to take its place in the canon of Scripture, never mind that the end result was a grotesque distortion of both the nature and the content of Scripture.

The response of the churches to this onslaught was decisive.

It also provided ample proof of the truth of 1 Cor. 11:19: 'For there must be also heresies among you, that they which are approved may be made manifest among you'. Marcion's attack on truth led directly to truth being more clearly defined and most doughtily defended. His deformed and stunted canon is, in fact, the first such list that we have. There was a virtually unanimous agreement among the churches about which books ought to be regarded as the authoritative Scripture. In spite of this, indeed because of it, no one had previously seen the need to list which books were Scripture. Now, in response to Marcion and his teaching, that commonly accepted canon was explicitly stated and defended. This earliest-surviving orthodox canon is usually called the Muratorian canon, after L.A. Muratori the antiquarian who discovered it in 1740. In addition 'anti-Marcionite' prologues to each of the four gospels were written, setting out the reasons for their inclusion in the canon of Scripture. They also vigorously defended the importance of the Acts of the Apostles, which was entirely discarded by Marcion.

The response to Marcion's ideas had a broader and more general implication. His teachings enjoyed considerable success and the evidence available to us suggests that he attracted a large number of followers. As a result, those doctrines that he particularly attacked had to be defined with greater care, and the Scriptural truth about these subjects was set out with greater and more scrupulous precision.

Despite its widespread condemnation Marcionism showed a surprising vitality and continued as a sort of alternative church for several centuries. Even when Marcionism proper died out, some of his ideas endured, and Marconian-like heresies have continued to crop up throughout the history of the church.

In particular, the contemporary relevance of this second century attack on Scripture is all too sadly evident. Though many of the claims made by so-called Higher Critics of a past century have been revealed as the unscholarly and unscientific falsehoods that they undoubtedly were, there are not wanting those who would leave us with less than 'the faith which was once delivered to the saints' (Jude 1:3). We need not look as far as the blasphemous excesses of the Jesus seminar, where theologians meet to decide, with a supreme arrogance which would be ludicrous if it were not so appallingly blasphemous, to decide which of the words of Christ recorded in the gospels were actually spoken by the Lord Jesus. We find a Marcion-like tendency wherever any portion of God's word is placed off-limits, wherever all of the Bible is not allowed its appropriate place of authority. And we need to guard against it in our own lives. While we would never dream of mutilating our Bibles, never dream of drawing a red pen – or a penknife – through the words of Scripture, we need constantly to guard against ignoring or disregarding any portion or part of the word of God. We need it all and, if we wish to bear faithful testimony to Christ, we must be prepared to take heed to 'all the counsel of God' (Acts 20:27).

CHAPTER 8

Montanus and the Attack on the Sufficiency of Scripture

In the previous chapter we saw how Marcion's heresy had attempted to prune the Bible, to leave God's people shorn of the word of God in its fulness. That offensive was repelled, but Satan is nothing if not a flexible enemy. Marcion's assault had scarcely been beaten back before the direction of the attack shifted dramatically. It was not now a subtraction from Scripture that troubled the churches, but addition to it by prophets who claimed that their utterances had an authority equal to that of the word of God.

It is clear from the New Testament that prophecy had played an important part in revealing the will of God in the first decades of the church age. Before the canon of Scripture was complete, those with the gift of prophecy were used by God to communicate with believers. However, that gift was time limited. Even in the earliest of the books of the New Testament, we are told that prophecy was 'about to cease', rendered superfluous by the arrival of 'that which is perfect' (I Cor. 13:8-10), the complete Word of God.

Church history confirms this – the gift of prophecy appears to have scarcely outlived the apostolic era. Thus, the emergence, towards the end of the second century, of a self-proclaimed prophet who presented his utterances as the authentic word of God was met by widespread concern and condemnation.

The prophet in question was a Phrygian named Montanus. Soon after his conversion from paganism, he moved among the churches in Asia Minor, claiming to be a prophet in receipt of direct revelation from God. These prophecies came, he claimed, through the inspiration of the Paraclete. This title drew on Christ's promise regarding the Holy Spirit in John 14:16: ' I will pray the father, and He shall give you another comforter [*paraclete*]' , but Montanists seem eventually to have regarded the Paraclete as a separate entity from the Holy Spirit. The manner of his prophecies was spectacular – he fell first into a trance and progressed to an ecstatic frenzy, in which he spoke as God. These utterances, he claimed, superseded the content and teaching of Scripture. The records of his prophecy suggest that Montanus himself was not especially interested in doctrinal innovation, though he did lay great emphasis on the importance of an ascetic mode of life.

Crucially, though, Montanus taught that Scripture could be added to. He soon built up a following of others who claimed to be inspired with revelations from God. Most prominent amongst these were two women, Priscilla and Maximilla who travelled with Montanus. As his teaching spread, it quickly became clear that Montanism was an attack not just on Scripture but also on the authority of the leaders of individual churches. As the seriousness of this challenge became clear, Montanus and his leading followers were excommunicated as heretics. A contemporary report suggests that Montanus and Maximilla ultimately hanged themselves. After their deaths, the heresy that they had initiated continued to grow, with ever more prophets offering ever more extravagant prophecies and ever less scriptural teaching. The extent of their deviation from Scripture can be seen in the words of one prominent follower who argued that 'the Paraclete published through Montanus more than Christ revealed in the Gospel, and not only more, but also better and greater things.' Montanism would ultimately become more than a niche heresy. It even counted among its members Tertullian who had been a prominent orthodox theologian in the early church. It continued to trouble the church through to the sixth century, when the emperor

Justinian ordered the destruction of the tombs of Montanus, Maximilla, and Priscilla, which had become shrines to their heretical teaching.

Without doubt, Montanism was a serious heresy. It was, however, most serious not for the content of the prophecies, but for the place it gave to prophecy. Montanus and his followers were explicitly saying that Scripture was not enough, that further additional revelation was essential to understanding the will of God. And, these revelations were not only additional to Scripture: in both content and delivery they were in emphatic contradiction to it.

As such, the emergence of Montanism posed a major challenge to the believers of the second century. Had the door to additional revelation been opened, faithful testimony for God would have become almost impossible. The emphatic and unified rejection of Montanus and his teachings, in spite of the prominent teachers who propagated them, was of crucial importance in the history of the church.

Sadly, the fight was not over. Satan is a persistent as well as a flexible opponent, and the nineteenth and twentieth centuries saw the emergence and the alarming spread of erroneous teaching that bears more than a passing resemblance to Montanus's. We do not have to search too hard or too long to find those who purport to receive special prophetic revelations from God, whether communicated in the throes of ecstatic frenzy or otherwise.

If, in conversation with these individuals, we point out the unscriptural nature of their experience and practice they will very likely accuse us of limiting the Spirit of God. His sovereign power, they contend, means that He can act as He chooses, move as He wills. In reality, the net result of their doctrine is not to glorify the Spirit: it is to undervalue – and indeed to devalue – the word of God. And the Holy Spirit cannot be glorified where the Scriptures that He inspired are set aside, disregarded, or added to.

The sufficiency of God's word is a remarkable truth. It means what it says – that the Bible is a sufficient guide for our Christian lives. Wonderfully God inspired His word in order that it might meet every need of His people. The words of the apostle Peter are relevant here: 'According as his divine power hath given unto us all things that pertain unto life and godliness, through the knowledge of him that hath called us to glory and virtue: Whereby are given unto us exceeding great and precious promises: that by these ye might be partakers of the divine nature, having escaped the corruption that is in the world through lust' (2 Pe.1:3-4). God has provided His people with everything that 'pertains to life and godliness', and the 'exceeding great and precious promises' of His word are central to that great provision.

We can, then, learn much from the example of the second century believers who recognized in the teaching of Montanus an intolerable heresy. We ought to be grateful that, by the grace of God, they stood firmly for the truth of God. In our day we cannot afford to do less.

CHAPTER 9

The Christological Debates

In chapter 11 of Second Corinthians Paul expresses his care for the believers to whom he wrote, and his urgent awareness of the error that they were about to face. Assuring them that he was jealous over them 'with a Godly jealousy' (v.2) he highlights – with unerring accuracy – the nature, of that attack:

> 'For if he that cometh preacheth another Jesus, whom we have not preached, or if ye receive another spirit, which ye have not received, or another gospel, which ye have not accepted, ye might well bear with him.' (v.4)

The English translation tends to obscure the vitally important point that the apostle is making. 'Another Jesus' is *allos* – another of the same sort – but 'another gospel' and 'another spirit' are *heteros* – others of a different sort. That point is crucial – there can be no minor differences in doctrine relating to the person of Christ. No matter how similar to the Scriptural standard another Jesus may seem, if he is not the Jesus of the Bible both the gospel that presents him and the spirit behind that gospel are very far different from the truth of Holy Scripture, as inspired by the Holy Spirit.

Paul's warning had a clear and urgent relevance for the Corinthian believers. In the next two centuries, its relevance for every church and for every believer would become all too clear. The Christological truth that is at the very heart of Christianity was to become the subject of serious and sustained attack.

It would be more accurate to say that Biblical Christology came under two attacks, for heresy and the *hetero*-spirit that inspired it launched a pincer movement, attacking Biblical doctrine on two opposite fronts. One arm of the assault attacked the deity of Christ, another His true humanity. Between these two errors both equally pernicious, equally heterodox – the early believers had to navigate as they strove to remain true to God and to His Word.

Teaching that denied the true deity of Christ was nothing new. Throughout His ministry, the Jewish authorities' most vociferous opposition was aroused when He spoke of Himself as the Son of God. 'He makes Himself equal with God' (John 5:18) was their recurring complaint. Calvary only added to their opposition. Bad enough that an itinerant teacher should claim equality with God, still worse that such a claim should be made for a man whose execution was calculated to express the deepest opprobrium of the Jewish and the Gentile worlds, and of Heaven itself.

As the apostles faithfully preached the Christ that they had known, they too encountered opposition from those who were willing, perhaps, to admit that Jesus of Nazareth made some good points, but would not acknowledge that He was who He claimed to be – the eternal Son of the Eternal God. This view found two expressions early in the church age. One arose from Jewish Christianity. This was the heresy of the Ebionites. Members of this sect denied the eternity, the deity, and the sonship of Christ. Anticipating the heretical teaching of many false religious teachers in our own day, they argued that Jesus was an outstandingly righteous man, chosen by God to be a special prophet, chosen to be the Messiah, but nonetheless a created being, and not truly God. A similar view was expressed by those who are known as Arians, followers of an Egyptian named Arius. Arian teachers had a higher view of Christ than the Ebionites. They acknowledged Him as the Son of God, but denied His eternal existence and His equality with the Father. It has been said their teaching came within an iota of being

Scriptural. They taught that Christ was *homoioúsios* – of a similar substance to God – not that He was *homooúsios* – of the same substance as God. Theirs was truly another Jesus, and for some such differences may well have seemed like trifling details. But much hung upon that one letter, and for all the similarity of the Christ that they presented, their teaching was heretical and represented a serious affront to the truth of God's word.

While heresy of this sort presented another Christ who was less than Divine, other teachers presented a Christ who was less than fully human. This teaching was primarily Greek in its origins. The idea that matter was inherently evil was deeply embedded in Greek philosophy. Had that notion remained in the sphere of philosophy it might, however mistaken, not have done a very great deal of damage. Imported into Christianity, though, its impact was alarming. And, as the prevailing philosophies of the society in which we live have the power to influence us far more than we imagine, it was inevitable that this idea would have just such an impact.

To those who had been influenced by Greek philosophy the idea of incarnation – that a transcendent God would really become man – was unthinkable. Surely, they reasoned, God would not soil Himself by association with matter. On this assumption were built two strands of gnostic heresy. One, called Docetism, from the Greek word meaning 'to seem', suggested that Christ's human form was an illusion – that His body did not have any real physical being. The other strand, termed Monarchianism or adoptionism, taught that a man named Jesus was taken over and controlled by the Divine essence at His baptism. A later development of this sort of teaching was Monophysitism, meaning one nature, which taught that the Incarnate Christ had only a Divine, and not a human nature. Each of these teachings, and others closely relating to them, had the ultimate effect of denying the reality of the incarnation, and undermining the teaching of Scripture concerning the genuine and actual humanity of the one who was 'manifest in flesh' (1 Tim. 3:16).

Whether these *hetereo* teachers presented another Christ who was less than Divine or less than human, they represented an assault on the very heart of Christianity. As their teaching gained popularity, the foundation of the gospel – the preaching of Christ crucified – was coming under attack. Such a serious attack had to be repelled, and the only thing that could repel it was the truth of God's word. And it was to that irresistible force that God's people turned.

Controversy about the nature of Christ, and especially about the Arian heresy, raged throughout the Roman Empire in the opening decades of the fourth century. This controversy threatened the peace of the Empire and so the Emperor Constantine called an international council of church leaders. Some 300 bishops gathered in Nicaea in the year 325. They did not gather to invent Christianity's teaching about the Lord Jesus Christ. Rather, they came to compare the Christology of different groups to the truth of Scripture and the teaching of the apostles. Arius himself attended, with 22 supporting bishops. But as passages from his writings were read, these supporters quickly deserted him, and the statement that resulted from the Council was all but unanimous. That statement has been passed down to us as the Nicene Creed. It summarizes the teaching of Scripture regarding the unity of God, the person and work of Christ, and the Holy Spirit. It repudiates the stunted Christology of the Arians, and represents the triumph of the truth of God's word over the preachers of 'another gospel'.

That triumph was neither final nor total. While the denial of Christ's deity and the threat posed by Arian heresy had been dealt with at Nicaea, the churches continued to be troubled by denials of Christ's true humanity, especially by the Monophysite heresy, which suggested that the Lord Jesus had only a Divine and not a human nature. In response to the continuing propagation of this view, church leaders gathered in Chalcedon in the year 451. There they produced a further statement of faith, which affirmed what we know as the hypostatic union of the Divine and human in the incarnate Christ. The creed produced by the Council, affirmed belief in 'our Lord Jesus Christ, the same perfect in Godhead and also perfect in manhood; truly God and truly man, of a reasonable [rational] soul and body; consubstantial with the Father according to the Godhead, and consubstantial with us according to the Manhood; in all things like unto us, without sin'.

Again it is important to understand that the council of Chalcedon was not inventing an orthodox Christology. Nor did their approval make the Christology embodied in the creed orthodox. Rather, they were addressing the challenge of doctrinal innovation by returning to the truth of God's word. And, while we look to Scripture and not to any human formulation as the basis of our faith we do well to take note of the truth stated and defended at Chalcedon. Heresy in our day has not ceased to repackage the erroneous teachings and other gospels of past centuries. We do well to heed the warning of the apostle and the instruction of history and to hold fast to 'the simplicity that is in Christ' (2 Cor. 11:3).

CHAPTER 10

The Bible in Latin:
Jerome and the Vulgate

In previous chapters, we saw how God overruled the spread of the Greek empire, culture, and language to prepare the world for the spread of the gospel and the teaching of the apostles. The Septuagint translation of the Hebrew Old Testament into Greek, and the fact that the New Testament was originally written in Greek meant that the Scriptures were accessible throughout the classical world.

The ascendency of the Greek empire did not last for long, however. Already by the time of the gospels, the Greek empire had fallen, and Roman rule spread over the greater part of the known world. The Latin language of Rome was slower to displace Greek as the most widely spoken language, but over time it began to dominate. To new generations who spoke Latin, the Greek scriptures were not accessible. This problem was addressed by a large number of translations of parts of the Bible into Latin. These translations had accumulated over more than a century, were incomplete in their coverage and very patchy in their quality. With time it became apparent a better and more complete translation was required.

In 382, this problem was recognized by Pope Damascus I, who commissioned Eusebius Hieronymous, better known as Jerome, to begin work on a new translation of Scripture into Latin. Jerome's parents were Christians, and, after being educated in Rome, Jerome was baptized, and lived a life of self-denial. However, the death of two of his friends, a serious illness, and a dream in which Christ said 'you are not a Christian' seem to have brought about Jerome's true conversion. After spending some time in the desert, and acquiring an excellent knowledge of both Greek and Hebrew, Jerome returned to Rome. Soon, his forthright criticism of the Roman church and the lax living of the Roman Christians resulted in his being asked to leave the city. He moved to Bethlehem, which provided him with an excellent base for translating the Hebrew Old Testament into Latin.

Initially, Jerome had been commissioned simply to revise the text of the existing Latin translation of the four gospels, but the project continued to grow until Jerome had overseen the translation of all of the Old Testament and most of the New. Not all of the work of translation was carried out by Jerome and, in some places, the new translation was more of a revision of existing Latin translations. The division of this work was based on Jerome's recognition that not all the books regarded as Scripture by the Catholic Church were inspired. He was probably the first person to use the term Apocrypha to describe the portions of the Septuagint that are not the translation of Hebrew originals. These, he clearly said, did not form part of the canon of Scripture. He was happy to leave the translation of these works to others, but translated the 39 books of the Hebrew Old Testament himself.

In addition to his translations, Jerome provided prologues to a number of Old Testament books, the Gospels, and to the Epistles of Paul among which, he argued, the Epistle to the Hebrews was to be numbered.

In contrast to the variable standard of the Old Latin translations that had been in use, Jerome's translation was of a high literary quality and, while not a closely literal translation, was still an accurate translation of Scripture into the Latin whose use had become widespread. Jerome valued the Hebrew manuscripts of the Old Testament very highly, and, while earlier Latin translations had been based on the Septuagint, his translation went back to the Hebrew text.

Latin was widely spoken throughout the Roman Empire and, even when that Empire crumbled, Latin remained in widespread use throughout Europe. Therefore, Jerome's translation was widely used throughout the Middle Ages, and, consequently, became known as the *versio vulgata*, or the Vulgate. In 1546, it was declared the official Bible of the Catholic Church by the Council of Trent and, though it has since been revised, it remains so.

Although Jerome's translation was in the common language of fifth century Europe and although the Vulgate was intended to make Scripture widely accessible, it came, ultimately, to have the opposite effect. To some extent, Jerome had done his job too well. Because his translation was so good, no one felt the need to improve it, and throughout the Middle Ages, the Vulgate remained the version of Scripture most widely used. As Latin became increasingly the language of the learned, those who did not speak it found themselves cut off from Scripture. Attempts to translate the Bible into the vernacular languages spoken by the common people of the European countries were opposed – often violently – by the priests who had come to see their monopoly on interpreting and expounding the meaning of Scripture as one of the chief sources of their power. It was, perhaps, this abuse more than any other that energized the Reformers in their protest against the Catholic Church.

The Vulgate was, for its day, an excellent translation. But it also reminds us that it is a dangerous and a foolish thing to insist that any one translation is the definitive version of the word of God. The words of Scripture are inspired; Jerome and his successors as translators of the Word were not. In medieval Europe, a project initially designed to make Scripture reliably and widely available ended up as the symbol of an exclusive and elitist approach to Scripture. And it may be that that irony is one of history's lessons for us.

CHAPTER 11

Translation and Reformation

To the non-expert, watching a game of chess can be a baffling experience. The pieces are moved to and fro, apparently at random. It is often only at the end of the game that we realise that what seemed random was, in fact, carefully planned by a player who was meticulously working towards the end he had in view.

In a similar way, one of the great joys of history, for the believer, is the way in which it allows us, with the benefit of hindsight and the luxury of a comprehensive view of events, to trace the way in which God orchestrates events to accomplish His purposes, to see in the apparently haphazard movements of people and events a wealth of providential foresight and an inexorable plan.

We have already noticed, in an earlier chapter, that the rise of the Macedonian empire and the consequent spread of the Greek language prepared the way for the apostles to spread the gospel. In the fifteenth and sixteenth centuries, God used very different events to prepare the way for the recovery of Scripture and the Reformation of the church. It is not an historical accident that the events of the Reformation were preceded by the European Renaissance.

When we think of the Renaissance, we often think of the paintings of Giotto, the sculptures and frescos of Michelangelo, and the inventions of Leonardo da Vinci. As a cultural 're-birth', the artists of the Renaissance looked back to the glories of the Classical period, which had been lost throughout the Middle Ages. But the renewal of the visual arts that took place in southern Europe was far from being the only – or the most important – manifestation of the Renaissance. As the Renaissance moved into northern Europe, its focus moved from paint to ink, from the visual arts to the study of texts.

Ultimately, it was the emergence of humanist philology that was the most significant result of the Renaissance. We think of humanism today as a God-less secular religion. In the Renaissance period, however, the term has a very different significance. Humanists were scholars who used the emerging techniques of linguistic and textual scholarship to better understand mankind and the world. Their efforts were directed into many subjects, but it was in the field of philology – the study of language, grammar, and texts – that they made the greatest advances.

Throughout the Middle Ages, the knowledge of Greek and Hebrew had been largely lost in Europe. Anti-Semitism and a general distrust of Jews had resulted in their expulsion from every European country, except for Italy, which had a sizable and educated Jewish community. Knowledge of Greek had become rare in western Europe, where Latin had become the scholarly *lingua franca*. Along with the language, many classical texts in Greek had been lost, and were unknown, or known only in summary or translation.

In 1453, this began to change. In that year, Constantinople, the capital city of the Byzantine empire fell to the troops of the Ottoman empire. Scholars fleeing from the invading troops brought a wealth of Hellenic knowledge with them into western Europe. This injection of new texts, and the learning that made them accessible, reignited enthusiasm for the Greek language. Towards the end of the fifteenth century, some of the major scholars of the Reformation had turned their attention to Hebrew language and culture, overcoming formidable obstacles to learn Hebrew. Often their motives were esoteric in the extreme, but the scholarship they produced – including glosses, lexicons, and textbooks – was of enormous value.

These developments meant that scholars now had the tools for the return *ad fontes*. This involved going back to the original sources of texts, back beyond translations and copies, to get as close to the original text as possible. This principle was applied to a wide range of texts, but it had its deepest and most important impact when applied to the Scriptures.

We have already seen how the Vulgate, Jerome's translation of Scripture into Latin, had become the definitive version of the Bible. We get a clear indication of the exalted status of the Vulgate in the preface to the Complutensian Polyglot, a critical edition of Scripture that featured parallel printings of the Vulgate, the Hebrew text, and the Greek text. The editors compared the Vulgate text, flanked by other versions with the crucified Christ in the midst of the thieves. Incredibly, those 'thieves' were Scripture in its original language. Jerome's Latin translation was being accorded a greater importance than he would have claimed for it.

Jerome had done an excellent job in his translation, over the centuries more manuscripts had been recovered, and, through transmission, the text of the Vulgate had become corrupt in many places.

Scripture, then, was an ideal candidate for the application of philology. Such was the regard in which the Vulgate was held, however, that scholars were slow to scrutinize it, and slower still to publish the results of that scrutiny. The Dutch scholar Desiderius Erasmus (1466 – 1536) was the first to brave the ire of churchmen and critics. Though Erasmus lived and died a Catholic, and although he was eventually to oppose the reformation, he was fully aware of the corruption of the Roman church and longed to see her purified. He believed that a Bible cleansed of error was an important part of purifying the church. He displayed a keen sense of the shortcomings of the Vulgate complaining that 'often through the translator's clumsiness or inattention the Greek has been wrongly rendered; often the true and genuine reading has been corrupted by ignorant scribes, which we see happen every day, or altered by scribes who are half-taught and half-asleep.' Erasmus examined all the manuscripts of the Vulgate that he could lay his hands on. He was careful not to suggest that he was replacing Jerome's work, stating 'We do not tear up the *Vulgate* ... but we point out where it is depraved, giving warning in any case of flagrant error on the part of the translator, and explaining it where the version is involved or obscure.' Crucially, though, he also examined the Greek manuscripts that were available to him and when his translation, the *Novum Instrumentum,* was published in 1516, it appeared as a parallel edition. Thus, those with the necessary expertise could verify Erasmus' Latin translation by examining the Greek text printed on the facing page.

It is significant that, while Erasmus used the more conventional title *Novum Testamentum* for subsequent editions, this first published Greek New Testament was described as an instrument. The title was a play on words – in legal terminology a testament was a type of instrument. But the choice of title also emphasized Erasmus' ambitions for his translation. He hoped that it would become a tool for translators of Scripture into the vernacular languages of Europe, fulfilling his vision that 'the husbandman, the smith, and the weaver' might read Scripture without difficulty.

Erasmus' work aroused a good deal of controversy. His temerity in daring to differ from the Latin of the Vulgate was widely denounced. But he had provided a vital tool, which would be wielded in the hands of the Reformers to tremendous effect. Luther's translation of the New Testament into German, and Tyndale's into English all relied heavily on the Greek text produced by Erasmus, and this text, the so-called *Textus Receptus* underpinned every Bible produced for more than a century after.

Other humanists followed Erasmus' example, and provided scholarly Latin translations of the Old Testament. The work of Sebastian Münster, Leo Jud, and Immanuel Tremellius produced translations that were of great use to succeeding generations of vernacular translators, but also provided a large amount of scholarly works that provided Latin-speaking students with access to the riches of Hebrew Scripture.

So it was that God, in His sovereign power, used alike the fall of a mighty empire and the skill and dedication of a single scholar to achieve His purpose. In the century that followed, Scripture would be set free of its Latin shackles, and would reach the hearts of men and women in their mother tongue. The ability to appeal directly to Scripture undermined the power of the Catholic church and her clergy, and changed the face of Christendom forever.

CHAPTER 12

The Reformation and the Recovery of *Sola Scriptura*

In the Church of All Saints in Wittenberg, Germany, the ritual of the Roman Catholic church was in full swing. The air swirled with the scented smoke of incense, almost obscuring the statues and images that lined the walls of the building and its magnificent vaulted ceiling. From the high altar came the musical drone of the Latin mass. From all over the building came the clack of rosaries and the murmur of prayer, interrupted only when the tinkle of a golden bell drew the adoring gaze of the congregation to the elevated host, a sacrifice that they could look at but not partake of. The wealth and error that the church had acquired through the Middle Ages was on display, a vast religious machine smoothly turning souls into money, ever adding to its wealth and prestige. But suddenly a new sound was heard – simple but portentous, cutting through the sonorous hum that filled the air, startling the priest and the people, and halting the liturgy in its well-worn track. It was the sound of nails being driven into the hard oak of the massive cathedral door. That sound would echo beyond the walls of Wittenberg till the whole world rang with it.

In reality the scene that took place when Martin Luther nailed his Ninety Five Theses (or topics for discussion) to the door of the cathedral was probably less dramatic – nailing a notice to the door was an established means of initiating public debate. But it is difficult to over-estimate the repercussions of Luther's action. Though only a humble monk, he was to become the piece of grit that brought the well-oiled machinery of the Catholic church almost to a standstill, that sowed consternation and alarm amongst the princes and prelates of Europe, and that brought light and hope to their benighted and despairing peoples. In this mission Luther was not motivated by political ambition or by religious fanaticism. Rather, he was impelled by the word of God. It was the study of Scripture that had brought him to faith in Christ. It was in its pages that he discovered that 'the just shall live by faith'. And, it was to Scripture that he appealed as he stood before the hostile Diet of Worms, saying 'my conscience is captive to the Word of God … here I stand, I can do no other, may God help me.'

Direct appeal to the authority of God's word does not, perhaps, seem a remarkable thing to us. But in Luther's day it was both radical and revolutionary. Throughout the Middle Ages the Roman Catholic church had done everything it could to declare scripture off-limits, and to replace it with the traditions of the church and the decrees of the papacy. Indeed, that trend had commenced before the Middle Ages. The church at Rome had always been prominent – a sort of first among equals. That position was based on the respect of believers for the doctrinal strength and the faithfulness of the believers in Rome. At the conversion of Constantine, however, the Roman church gained a political power that was far from Scriptural. As such power does, this new importance quickly corrupted the Roman church, which developed territorial ambitions to match those of the Empire with which she was now identified. And because Scripture that was freely available and open to all would not serve these ambitions, the place and power of the Word of God was undermined and circumscribed by the teaching of the Roman church.

This attack involved three strategies. Firstly, the Roman church claimed a monopoly on the correct interpretation of Scripture. Only the teachings of the doctors of the church, and ultimately of the Pope could be regarded as definitive. This teaching authority, vested in the hierarchy of the Roman Catholic church is called the Magisterium, and it is still the teaching of that church that 'The task of interpreting the Word of God authentically has been entrusted solely to the Magisterium of the Church, that is, to the Pope and to the bishops in communion with him.' This teaching cut believers off from the word of God, it denied them the opportunity to emulate the noble Bereans who 'received the word with all readiness of mind, and searched the scriptures daily, whether those things were so', and it meant that the church had tremendous power to control the way in which Scripture was to be understood.

This attempt to monopolize the interpretation was bolstered by the way in which the Church opposed the translation of Scripture into the vernacular languages of the European peoples. The intent of Jerome's Vulgate, in providing a new translation of the Hebrew and Greek of the Bible into Latin, had been to make Scripture widely and accurately available. In a world where there was no longer an overlap between literacy and the ability to understand Latin, the use of the Vulgate further empowered the church, and further disempowered those who might otherwise have been too aware of the growing divide between the teachings of the Apostles, and those of the Roman church. Some access to vernacular Scripture remained in glosses and lectionaries, and some – both priests and laymen – continued faithfully to preach the truth of God's Word. But there were many whose only knowledge of Scripture was dependant on the teaching of the church.

In its drive for power, wealth, and dominion, the papacy did not wish to be limited to 'the faith which was once delivered unto the saints' (Jude v.3), or even to Scripture as interpreted by the pope. So, the concept of the unwritten word of God was developed. The dogmatic pronouncements of the popes and doctors of the church had the same force and effect as the teaching of the apostles. If the political or financial interests of the Roman church needed the support of doctrine, the pope could provide it.

Thus, through the Middle Ages, was scripture side-lined, locked away from the people, interred in a strange language, and belittled by the introduction of new dogmas. Believers in this period had no way of evaluating the truth of what they heard from their priest, no way of knowing when innovative doctrine was being foisted upon them. They simply had to take on trust the teaching of the Roman Catholic church, and to accept the proposition that the pope knew best.

It is in this context that the true significance of Luther's action must be understood. Along with the other reformers, Luther's teaching had an influence on the way in which all sorts of doctrines were understood. But his return to Scripture was the most important, most fundamental, and most radical of all his contributions to the health of the church. *'Sola scriptura'*, 'Scripture alone' became one of the great watch cries of the Reformation. Luther in Germany, Tyndale in England, Olivetan in France, and Diodati in Italy began the translation of Scripture into the vernacular languages of Europe. Scripture once again became widely read and widely discussed, in the markets and the taverns as well as in the schools and universities. Volumes of Biblical commentary began to pour from the presses. Like a mighty river, the torrent of Scripture swept through Europe, washing away the accumulated junk of centuries, undermining the power of the papacy, bringing truth and its sister freedom to those who had sat in great darkness.

We look to Scripture, and not to the Reformers, for our doctrine. Nonetheless, we should thank God for those who were raised up by Him to restore His word to its rightful place as the only source and final arbiter of spiritual truth. And these men have a great deal to teach us. They were, in Luther's memorable phrase, captives to the word of God. They were prepared to put everything – wealth, safety, and life itself – on the line in order to stand for its truth against human traditions. We need to maintain a similar attitude to God's word. We ought not to oppose tradition simply because it is tradition. But we should never obey tradition when it is in contradiction with the teachings of Scripture. Moreover, we must be always on our guard lest we imitate the Pharisees who were upbraided by the Lord Jesus because they taught 'for doctrines the commandments of men' (Matthew 15:9). May God help us to live the truth of *sola scriptura*, individually and as assemblies of His people.

CHAPTER 13

The Reformation
and Justification by Faith

The Epistle to the Romans is the beating heart of the gospel. In it, as nowhere else in Scripture, the doctrines of this most glorious message are comprehensively surveyed. In the pages of this epistle the Holy Spirit takes us down into the depths of human depravity and up again to that tremendous peak where we learn of God's purpose that members of that fallen race should ultimately and inevitably be 'conformed to the image of His Son' (Rom. 8:29). And, at the heart of this remarkable letter is the truth – simple, yet world-shatteringly profound – 'the just shall live by faith' (Rom. 1:17).

In the epistle Paul describes the gospel as the revelation of the righteousness of God' (1:17). Things that we could never have guessed about God and His character are made known to us uniquely in this great message. The great principle of justification by faith – or, more comprehensively and correctly, justification by grace alone, through faith alone, in Christ alone – is one of those Scriptural truths that would have been inaccessible to us apart from God's revelation of it in His Word. That man is depraved may be clearly seen. That God is great and good may be inferred from the general revelation of His person and His power in the natural creation. But the fact that He would choose this way of justifying sinners lies well beyond the grasp of our instincts or our intellects. The gospel is unique in its dependence upon what God has done. Man, and every religion he has ever devised and designed, is fixated on what he can do. Paul laid an unerring finger on the root of this obsession when he emphasised that salvation is 'not of works, lest any man should boast' (Eph 2:9). We love to boast, and are constitutionally opposed to the idea that there is nothing that we can bring to God, no work that we can do, no way in which we may cooperate with Him in the salvation of our souls.

That attitude is natural – an integral part of the thinking of unsaved men and women. And, like any natural fault, it has the potential to affect even those who are saved. The apostle Paul, for example, wrote with a remarkable vehemence to warn the Galatian believers who were in danger of being seduced from reliance on the sufficiency of Christ. In the second chapter he reminds them of what they already knew: 'Knowing that a man is not justified by the works of the law, but by the faith of Jesus Christ, even we have believed in Jesus Christ, that we might be justified by the faith of Christ, and not by the works of the law: for by the works of the law shall no flesh be justified' (2:16). A little later he drives the point home still further: 'Are ye so foolish? having begun in the Spirit, are ye now made perfect by the flesh?' (3:3).

The erroneous doctrines that Paul addressed with such urgency in Galatians may have withered beneath his words, but they did not die. Right from the first century of church testimony, there were those found who preached a salvation partially, if not wholly, based upon or sustained by the righteous works of the individual. Their gospel – another of a different sort, and not of the same (Gal 1:6-7) – had an appeal to the human desire to work and to boast and, its popularity increased as the centuries passed, and the church moved toward ages that, as far as the gospel light was concerned, were dark indeed. That darkness was deep: it was not absolute. There were still believers, saved by grace, through faith, and still those who taught that truth to others. One such man was an Augustinian monk named Johann van Staupitz. When Staupitz met a troubled young monk named Martin Luther, who was deeply conscious of his sinfulness, and seeking by any means to find release he pointed him not to the importance of good works, or the merits of church or sacrament but to the work accomplished by Christ on the cross. Luther was later to remark 'Staupitz lighted the flame of the gospel for me. Without [him] I would rather be in hell than in heaven'.

Luther, and the Reformation in which he played such an important role, would famously insist on the fundamental importance of *sole fide, sole gratia* – justification by grace alone through faith alone. But the reformers were doing more than preaching the truth of justification by faith as it had been understood in past centuries. Luther and his brilliant friend Philipp Melanchthon carefully studied the Scriptures in light of the most recent advances in the understanding of Biblical Greek. As they did so, they came to understand a vital distinction that had often been overlooked. This was the difference between justification and sanctification. In Catholic teaching, justification was the process by which the sinner was made righteous before God. As Melanchthon scrutinised Scripture, and especially the epistle to the Romans, he came to understand that justification was not a process of improvement by which a sinner was made righteous. Rather, it was a judicial act by which God declared a sinner righteous. That justification was followed by a process of sanctification, but this was the working out of a right position before God, and not a means to achieving it.

The recovery of this scriptural truth was of enormous significance. It restored the true meaning of Christian freedom, as souls no longer lived a righteous life in order to rack up spiritual Brownie points. Rather, a godly life became the privilege of the justified soul, the glad response of the liberated heart, and the practical working out of a right standing obtained through faith in Christ. Part of the purpose of the Saviour's work at Calvary was to 'deliver them who through fear of death were all their lifetime subject to bondage' (Heb. 2:15). Now, as the truth of the gospel was rediscovered, that liberty was brought to fruition in the experience of countless souls.

This understanding of the doctrine of justification became fundamental to the Reformation. It was not the only concern of the Reformers, nor did all of them understand its significance in the same way. Nonetheless, they were united in their commitment to salvation by grace alone, through faith alone, in Christ alone, *Sola Fides, Sola Gratia*. And for that we ought to be deeply thankful. We claim these men neither as leaders or founders. We do not uncritically accept their teaching, nor claim that, in every detail, it accords with the Word of God. But we must give God thanks for those who bought the truth and did not sell it (Prov. 23:23) but who stood fast for it in the face of formidable opposition.

We should also note well the way in which the truth of Scripture was recovered. Melanchthon's recovery of the truth was not the result of casual reading. He did not find it in his daily reading book, nor was it a challenging thought discovered in a verse detached from its context. He discovered the truth through the careful, painstaking study of the word of God. To that study he brought every natural talent. He applied the outstanding education that he had received. The fruits of that effort transformed Christendom, and placed us for ever in his debt.

His example is important for us. This generation is more – if not always better – educated than any that has gone before. We have experience of applying our minds with diligence and discipline to complicated and challenging subjects. We have the benefit of training in critical and analytical thinking. Daily we use these skills in our work, laying them at the disposal of our earthly employer. Too often, we seem to abandon them at the closet door, and approach Scripture in a haphazard and disorganised way. God and His Word deserve better, and in the story of the Reformation we see writ large the value and importance of Paul's exhortation: 'Study to show thyself approved unto God: a workman that needeth not to be ashamed, rightly dividing the word of truth' (2 Tim 2:15).

CHAPTER 14

'Truth will conquer' – John Wycliffe and the English Bible

How many Bibles do you own? For very few of us would the answer to that question be 'one.' We have Bibles on our shelves, in our pockets, on our laptops, and on our phones. There are Bibles for every price range: some may have cost us a great deal, others have not cost us anything. We have a choice of versions, a choice of printings, and can even choose the colour of our binding to match our shoes or our clothes. We are inundated by choice, and need never be without access to the Word of God.

But imagine that this was not so. Imagine that there was only one version of the Bible available to you. Imagine that a single copy of this Bible took ten months of skilled labour and a great deal of costly material and that, as a consequence, it cost £40, a sum of money which would have fed ten families for a year. Imagine further that this Bible, an enormous calf-bound book, had to be carefully hidden when not in use, because the mere possession of the Scriptures in English was punishable by death. Such a situation is difficult for us to understand but, in the fifteenth century, these were the obstacles that had to be faced and overcome by any Englishman or woman who wanted to read God's word in their mother tongue.

But at least fifteenth century believers could read the Scriptures in their own language. While partial translations of the Bible into English had been made in previous centuries, no complete English Bible had ever existed. That the need for such a translation was recognized and addressed owes a great deal to John Wycliffe (*c.*1330-1384) and, though it is likely that he did not translate any of the Bible that bears his name, it is fitting that the first English Bible has become known as the Wycliffe Bible.

John Wycliffe has justly been described as 'the morning star of the Reformation'. Over a century before Marin Luther nailed the Ninety-Five Theses to the door of Wittenberg cathedral, Wycliffe was a voice crying in the wilderness, lamenting and opposing the doctrinal error and moral abuses of the Roman Catholic Church. As a scholar at Oxford and a priest at Lutterworth, Wycliffe preached and wrote against a wide range of abuses in the Church. Primarily, he opposed Rome on three crucial issues. He objected to the authority that the Pope claimed in English affairs. At this time the Roman papacy exercised enormous power over the nations of Europe and claimed a power greater than that of King or parliament. Wycliffe argued for the sovereignty of the English nation, but also objected that, in making these claims to supranational authority, the Pope was displacing Christ – the King of kings. Wycliffe also took a stand against the Catholic doctrine of transubstantiation – the belief that, in the mass, the bread and wine were transformed into Christ's body and blood. Anticipating the later Reformers, Wycliffe dismissed this teaching as unscriptural, and this dismissal struck directly at the power of the priests. Perhaps the most significant of Wycliffe's quarrels with Rome, though, was over the issue of Scripture. In his book *The Truth of Holy Scripture*, Wycliffe taught that Scripture was without error and contained God's revelation in its entirety. This meant that Scripture alone was sufficient to guide the life of the believer and the church – no traditions of the fathers or pronouncements of the Pope were needed.

Wycliffe's views attracted to him a large number of people who were equally disenchanted with the state of the Church. Individuals from all social ranks accepted Wycliffe's teaching on the truth of Scripture. They played a vitally important role in spreading Wycliffe's ideas beyond the universities, traveling all over England preaching to the common people. Their emphasis on preaching in English led the clergy to label them, dismissively, as 'Lollards', or mumblers. It seems unlikely that this aspersion on their preaching is deserved: these men, who moved in danger of intense persecution or death, made a profound impact on English society.

But the most profound achievement of Wycliffe's life was the influence of his vision upon the translation of Scripture. The necessity for a translation followed naturally from his belief that Scripture was the one important standard for the Christian life. Wycliffe himself was, most probably, not directly involved in the translation project. Instead, the translation seems to have been started by Nicholas of Hereford. It was continued by a number of translators. Traditionally, it has been said that the translation was revised heavily by John Purvey, the 'Lollard librarian', whose signature can be seen in one of the Bibles in the collection of Trinity College Dublin. More recently, however, claims of Purvey's involvement have been questioned. Whoever was responsible for the translations, surviving Wycliffe Bibles fall into two main groups, representing an earlier and a later translation effort. Because Greek and Hebrew were virtually unknown in medieval England, these translations were based on the Latin Vulgate. By our standards, it is a stiff translation, and the adherence to the Latin word ordering in the earlier version especially, makes it difficult to read at times. Nonetheless, its significance was immense.

Distributing the Bible involved even greater challenges than its translation. Printing with moveable type had not yet been invented, so each Bible had to be copied out, slowly and painstakingly, by hand. This made the finished product very expensive. Few individuals could afford such a costly book, and there are records of people travelling considerable distances or paying large sums simply to hear the Bible read and to spend time with the Book.

But cost was only one of the obstacles to the spread of the

word of God in English. Wycliffe had challenged the authorities on a number of fronts and, in response, Archbishop Arundel drew up the Constitutions of Oxford in 1408. While the Church had always discouraged the possession of Scripture in the vernacular, these constitutions made it illegal for the first time, and introduced severe punishments for any association with the Lollards. As a result of these laws, many English Christians went to the stake or the gallows. Wycliffe was dead by this time but, rather than have him escape the stake, the Church ordered that his remains be exhumed and burned.

As well as burning Christians, the bishops burned Bibles. Any copies of the Wycliffe Bible found in the possession of Lollards were seized and destroyed. Despite this, over two hundred have survived. In these Bibles we have an ample testimony to the success and importance of Wycliffe's vision and to the determination of his followers that Scripture be restored to its unique position of authority. We owe him and them a deep debt of gratitude for their sacrifices and their commitment to the truth of the word of God.

CHAPTER 15

The Ploughboy's Bible – William Tyndale

The Matthew Bible, first published in 1537, was the first English Bible to be printed with official approval. Thanks largely to the skilled lobbying of Miles Coverdale, King Henry VIII had given it his royal approval. It is difficult to know how carefully the king had read the copy submitted to him by Coverdale. He seems to have missed or misunderstood the large and ornate W.T. that followed the end of Malachi. Had he recognised Coverdale's tribute to a notorious heretic executed just a few years earlier, he might have thought twice about giving his consent to this revolutionary project.

Such a tribute was well earned. Any history of the Reformation and any telling of the story of the English Bible would be incomplete if it did not pay attention to the remarkable life and work of William Tyndale, if it failed to acknowledge his towering intellect, steely determination, and total devotion to the truth of God's word.

Tyndale was born in Gloucestershire, England around 1494. His family were involved in the cloth trade. This, along with his place of birth, is significant: the clothiers of Gloucestershire were notorious for their Lollard or Wycliffite sympathies. It is not clear at what point Tyndale decided to give his life to the translation of Scripture but his upbringing seems almost certain to have been a vitally important factor and Tyndale's life work may, in a sense, be the most enduring legacy of John Wycliffe.

From Gloucestershire Tyndale went first to Oxford University and then to Cambridge. In both institutions he was identified with those who gathered to read and discuss the Scriptures. At this time Cambridge, in particular, was a hot bed for the teachings of Martin Luther, and included among its students some of the most influential figures of the English Reformation.

Tyndale left Cambridge early in the 1520s, and took a position as a tutor to the children of a wealthy Gloucestershire family. By this time he was firmly committed to the ideas of the Reformation and upset and annoyed many of the important local clerics who enjoyed his master's hospitality by the anti–clerical tone of his table talk. But the life work that he had chosen – to 'cause the boy that drives the plough to know more of the Scriptures than the Pope himself' – meant that he could not remain in his comfortable and congenial position.

The Constitutions of Oxford, which had been passed, we might recall, to suppress the Wycliffite movement, made it illegal to translate the Bible into English without the endorsement of a bishop. Tyndale, proceeding within the law, sought out Tunstall, the Bishop of London. Tunstall must have seemed a promising prospect – he was known as a scholarly and moderate cleric. However, he refused to approve Tyndale's proposal, and Tyndale realised that, if his work of translation were to be done, it would have to be done outside of England. So, for his country's blessing he went into exile, leaving England behind him for ever.

Germany seemed an obvious place to set up operations. Here, at the centre of Luther's teaching, Tyndale could find opportunity to begin the translation of Scripture. Furthermore, a location at one of the great European ports would make it easy to get the finished Bibles to England. And, just as importantly, printing technology in Germany and the Low Countries (the Netherlands) far surpassed anything available in England, So, after spending time in Hamburg and Wittenberg, Tyndale arrived in Cologne early in 1525.

His work prospered and, by the summer of 1525, he saw the first printed pages of the English Bible coming off the press. But there was little room for complacency. Cardinal Wolsey's network of spies had reported Tyndale's location and identity, and tipped off the Cologne authorities who raided the printers. Printing had reached as far as Matthew 22. Tyndale and his assistant just had time to flee, grabbing the printed sheets, and took off, up the Rhine to Worms. There the work continued and, in 1526, the first complete printing of the English New Testament was completed. The shift to Worms had had a profound and providential influence on the shape of the English New Testament. The Cologne printing had been a large and fairly ornate book modelled closely on Luther's September Testament. The complete Worms edition was smaller and simpler, but clearly printed: a book that could be easily used. Just as importantly, the book could readily be smuggled into England, often by those cloth merchants with whom Tyndale had lifelong links.

The availability of Scripture in English dismayed and alarmed Church authorities in England. Since the beginning of the European Reformation, books by Luther, Calvin, and other Reformers had been burned from time to time. To the horror of Tyndale and others, the Word of God was also put to the fire. Even this was used in the furtherance of Tyndale's work – some reports from the period suggest that Tunstall, now implacably opposed to Tyndale and his work, was sold Bibles for burning at inflated prices by Tyndale's supporters, who channelled the money raised back to Tyndale.

Tyndale's work continued. He was busy revising his translation of the New Testament, improving and refining his work. But he also moved to face new challenges. In spite of the complexity of finding a qualified teacher of Hebrew, and the difficulty of mastering Hebrew in his middle age, Tyndale began work on the translation of the Old Testament. The Pentateuch was published in 1530. Though Tyndale's translation of the historical books of the Old Testament was never published under his own name, it provided the basis for Coverdale's Old Testament. These books reveal his brilliance as a translator, especially when we realise how little was known about Hebrew during the early modern period.

We would give much to have Tyndale's translation of Old Testament poetry. But he was never to complete it. Tyndale was befriended by a man named Henry Philips. Philips, the wastrel son of a wealthy English family, acted as an agent for Wolsey and other powerful English clergy. He befriended Tyndale, entered into his confidence, and betrayed him to the authorities in Antwerp. Tyndale was charged with heresy and, in spite of intercession on his behalf by Thomas Cromwell (Henry VIII's pro–Reformation chief minister), was sentenced to death.

So it was that, in the early days of October 1536, one of the spiritual giants of the English Reformation was delivered by the ecclesiastical court to the secular authorities. Brought to the place of execution, he was tied to the stake amidst a pile of fire wood. Some little mercy was shown to him – he was strangled before the executioner's torch was laid to the wood. But before his breath was stopped, his final prayer restated the preoccupation of his life and expressed the desire of his heart. 'With a fervent zeal, and a loud voice' he cried 'Lord, open the King of England's eyes.'

Only eternity will reveal whether this prayer was answered in relation to Henry's personal salvation. Sadly it is very far from clear that it was. But Henry was soon to give his approval to the Coverdale Bible, and, within four years of Tyndale's death, four translations of the Bible, all drawing heavily on Tyndale's work, were in print in England. The progress of Reformation and the spread of the gospel in England would not, in the future, always be smooth. But, thanks to Tyndale's steadfast commitment and remarkable ability, the availability of Scripture in English was secured for the future. It is no small tribute to that zeal and ability that Tyndale's work has survived. The phrases he coined have become an integral part of the English language but, more than that, his work provided the backbone to English Bible translation for centuries to come.

CHAPTER 16

The Geneva Bible

'Lord, open the King of England's eyes!' Uttered from a bonfire in Antwerp, the dying prayer of William Tyndale asked not just for Henry VIII's personal enlightenment but for that of a nation. And, shortly after Tyndale's death, the light of the gospel began to shine more strongly in England. The spread of that light was slow and painful however. While English laypeople demonstrated their appetite for the word of God in their own language, their rulers were not always so enthusiastic. When Henry did eventually break from the Church of Rome, his reasons had far more to do with sovereignty – and his complicated family life – than with doctrine. Though his motivation may have been less than noble, his action in proclaiming that he, and not the Pope, was the head of the English church did allow those in his administration who favoured the cause of Reform to advance it. Such efforts required enormous diplomatic ability, but slowly the light grew.

After Henry's death in 1547, his only son, aged 9, ascended the throne as Edward VI. A council of regency initially ruled. This council was made up of reforming nobles, who accelerated the programme of reformation. As Edward began to exert his own influence, it became clear that his commitment to reformation went well beyond his father's. Under his reign, men like Thomas Cranmer had a new freedom to reform the practice of the Church. A number of Scriptural doctrines, including most importantly the truth of justification by faith alone, were adopted as official doctrines of the Church of England. But before the full extent of Edward's – and Cranmer's

– ambitions could be realised, the young king died, in 1553, at the age of 15.

Edward's death precipitated a succession crisis. The closest heir was his sister Mary, but she was ardently Catholic. Protestant nobles found their most promising candidate in Lady Jane Gray, Edward's cousin. She was in fact crowned queen, but after nine days was imprisoned by those loyal to Mary, and she and her husband were beheaded.

Thus it was that England, once more, had a Catholic monarch, Moreover, that monarch was determined to root out the shoots of reformation, and blot out the light of the gospel once more. In pursuit of this, she embarked on the vicious campaign of persecution that earned her the title 'Bloody Mary'. Many English Christians were tortured and slaughtered – at the stake, on the gallows, and at the pillory.

Fleeing such persecution, many other Christians left England for the European continent. Many of these 'Marian exiles' made their way to the city-state of Geneva, a theocratic society based, in large part, on the teachings of John Calvin and Theodore Beza. There, Beza had established the Geneva Academy, a university devoted to the humanities. This academy became a centre for the translation of Scripture into the European vernaculars: French, Italian, and Spanish. Here, too, work began on a new translation of the Bible into English. A small number of the English theologians and scholars gathered at Geneva began work on a new translation of the Scriptures, both for the benefit of English congregations on the continent and of their persecuted fellow-believers in England. The first edition of the New Testament in this translation was published in 1557 and the first edition of The Geneva Bible was published in 1560. In 1576 the first edition to be printed in England was published, and over 150 editions, in various revisions, were ultimately issued.

The Geneva Bible was heavily in debt to the past. Like every translation of Scripture before the twentieth century, it drew heavily on Tyndale's work. As a measure of this indebtedness, it is estimated that the Geneva Bible retains almost ninety percent of Tyndale's translation.

But the work of the Geneva translators was also innovative in many ways. The Geneva Bible was the first English Bible to have all of its Old Testament translated directly from Hebrew. It was the first English Bible to feature verse numbers as well as chapter numbers. While previous English Bibles had been printed in 'black letter' typefaces, the Geneva Bibles were set in modern Roman type. Words provided by the translators, to help with the English sense were printed in italic type for the first time in this Bible. This valuable new feature signalled how committed its translators were to the concept of the verbal inspiration of Scripture, and it was adopted, almost a century later, by the translators of the King James Bible.

These were important and useful innovations. They paled into relative insignificance, however, next to the Geneva Bible's most significant novelty. The Geneva translators did not just provide the world with a new English Bible, they produced the first ever study Bible.

The idea of including interpretative helps in the same volume as Scripture was not a new one. Printings of the Vulgate were available with all manner of helps, and both Luther and Tyndale's vernacular translations had included – sometimes at some length – prologues that guided the reader to a correct understanding of Scripture. But what was dramatically new was the decision of the Geneva translators to print their notes to Scripture alongside the passages that they expounded. These marginal notes, along with detailed woodcuts of the tabernacle, the garments of the High Priest, and other visual aids, provided the reader with Scripture and commentary in one convenient volume. This format has survived, and a quick scan of the shelves of any Bible bookshop will confirm its enduring popularity.

In spite of that popularity, it is not clear that the Geneva notes were an unmixedly good thing. Written as they were in Calvin's Geneva and by Calvinist theologians, they embodied a Calvinist understanding of Scripture. They were enormously effective in spreading these ideas – their influence, along with that of the returning Genevan exiles under Elizabeth changed the orientation of the English church from Luther's teachings to Calvin's. Our view of the value, or otherwise, of this effect will obviously depend greatly on our estimation of the value of that teaching.

In any case, the Geneva Bible's annotations were to some degree responsible for its ultimate demise. This demise came only after considerable success – for decades the Geneva Bible was the English Bible of choice, the Bible of Shakespeare, Spenser, and Donne. It was the Bible available in every church and in more and more households.

However, as the Calvinism of its notes became less popular with some parties within the English church, the Geneva Bible itself was regarded with increasing disfavour. Furthermore, Elizabeth's failure to produce an heir – or even to marry – meant that King James VI of Scotland became James I of England. James had, even for the time, an unusually exalted view of kingship, and the anti-monarchical orientation of some of the Geneva notes offended him. Ultimately, as we shall see, all parties within the English church agreed on the need for a new and entirely un-annotated translation.

The Geneva Bible was an important stage in the development of the English Bible. It was successful and hugely influential. Its weakness, however, was its notes, which caused Scripture itself to be seen as a partisan document. In the final analysis, this first study Bible is a cautionary tale about blurring the lines between the infallible and unfailing Word of the Living God, and the words of men, no matter how well intentioned those men or how helpful their words may be.

CHAPTER 17

King James and the
Hampton Court Conference

The 1611 King James Version of the Bible is often regarded as a timeless monument of Bible translation, the crowning achievement of English literature somehow remote from the influences of politics, doctrinal disagreement, or personal bias. This viewpoint, though appealing, is misleading. While the King James Version is, in truth, a fine translation and a remarkable literary achievement, while it occupies a unique position in the hearts of many of God's people, while it is, for many of us, 'our Bible' in a special way, it did not emerge in the undisturbed calm of an evangelical Utopia. Rather, its origins were complex and politically charged, and its success was by no means assured. In the providence of God, however, it did succeed, and the complicated and messy circumstances in which it had its roots served further its usefulness and enhance its value as a sound translation of God's word.

To understand the context in which the KJV had its origins we must pay attention to the events that were happening in England at the dawn of the seventeenth century. On March 24, 1603, Elizabeth I died. During her reign, the Church of England had been established as a moderately reformed church, Protestant in its doctrine, but retaining many of the ceremonies of the pre-Reformation church. This Elizabethan settlement, in trying to please everyone, had come to please no one and, at the time of the queen's death, two parties had emerged within the English Church. The majority party, certainly among the bishops, tended to favor an increased ceremonialism, emphasizing the role of the clergy and the importance of the sacraments. A sizeable minority – often described as puritans, though that is a problematic term in the English context – felt that the Elizabethan settlement had only commenced the work of the Reformation. They wanted a simpler and less ceremonial church, with a greater focus on preaching and with a less exalted view of the ordained ministry. Towards the end of Elizabeth's reign, these groups were at a stalemate – the aged queen seemed to have little interest in supporting either. Her death, however, opened up an exciting range of possibilities for both parties.

Elizabeth died unmarried and childless. There was, therefore, no direct heir to fill the English throne. The closest candidate was James VI of Scotland. His religious views were something of a puzzle. On the one hand, his mother had been the notoriously Catholic Mary, Queen of Scots, who had been executed on Elizabeth's orders. On the other, he had reigned Presbyterian Scotland effectively, seemingly getting on well with the ministers of the Scottish Kirk. Faced with such a conundrum, the leaders of both groups in the English church rushed to lobby the new king, and to secure his approval for their positions. The puritans didn't wait for James to arrive in London, but presented him with the 'Millenary Petition' during his slow progress southwards. The 'Millenary Petition' was a statement of puritan hopes for further reformation, reportedly signed by over a thousand ministers. It objected to those aspects of church practice that these ministers, and many English laypeople, regarded as unacceptable hangovers from Catholicism. In response to this petition, James called a conference of bishops, held at the magnificent Hampton Court Palace, for the discussion of these and other concerns.

James appears to have had a politician's ability to appear to promise everyone what they wanted, and then to do whatever he wanted personally. It quickly became clear to the puritan delegates at Hampton Court that they could expect little in the way of further reform from this new king. The four puritan delegates, who faced eighteen of the most illustrious members of the opposing party, failed to secure the king's endorsement for any of their positions. As the conference drew to a close, it seemed that they would enjoy no success, and extract no concessions from the new king.

However, in the last minutes of the last session, Dr John Reynolds, the leader of the puritan grouping made a suggestion. This, seemingly, came out of nowhere: it was no part of the Millenary petition or of the Conference's agenda. Whatever the reason, Reynolds called for a new translation of Scripture to be authorized by the King. Reynolds' proposal was greeted with the only unanimity the conference produced. The puritans liked his idea because it stressed the importance of Scripture. It also offered their only prospect of a positive result from the conference. The more ceremonially-minded bishops liked it because it offered the opportunity to replace the massively popular Geneva Bible, whose annotations did not sit well with their theology. And the king liked it. Probably the idea appealed to James for a number of reasons. He too was unhappy about some of the marginal notes of the Geneva Bible – less on theological grounds than on the basis that they seemed to undermine the absolute authority of the king and to legitimate the sort of action that had seen his mother deprived of her head. A newly authorized translation also allowed a unique opportunity for James to stamp his authority on the English church, and to offer something that would appeal to both parties within that church.

So it was that work began on the translation of Scripture variously (though inaccurately) known as the King James or the Authorized Version. The project proceeded quickly. Within six months fifty-four translators had been appointed. Only forty-seven of these actually worked on the translation. They were divided into six teams, two each located in Oxford, Cambridge, and Westminster. These panels included the leading experts in Hebrew and Greek, from across the doctrinal range of the English Church, from the ceremonially and sacramentally-focused Lancelot Andrews to the puritan John

Reynolds. We know very little about some of these men. Many of them held doctrinal positions that would occasion us considerable unease. They were, united, however in the conviction that the Bible was the inspired Word of God. These men were not inspired, nor was their work inerrant. But, over the next seven years, as they set aside doctrinal and personal differences to work on the new version of the Bible, they did accomplish a remarkable feat. In spite of circumstances that seemed scarcely propitious, they produced a translation of Scripture whose popularity and usefulness has endured over four centuries and that celebrated its four hundreth birthday as valuable as it ever was.

CHAPTER 18

The King James Version

As we have seen in the previous chapter, the fraught politics and ecclesiastical in-fighting that dominated the closing years of Elizabeth's reign were given clear expression at the Hampton Court conference. This event was convened to address the concerns of those who wanted the further reformation of the English church but ended in disappointment, as their requests were largely ignored or denied. It was in this atmosphere that the suggestion of a new translation of Scripture originated. It was hardly an auspicious start. Yet the translation of Scripture that resulted from John Reynold's last minute suggestion was one of the greatest achievements of the English Reformation, one of the most enduring monuments of English literature, and the best loved English translation of Scripture. The Authorized or King James Version, as it came, with questionable accuracy, to be known occupies a unique place in the history of the English Bible. In the centuries that followed its translation, it helped to form the fabric of English language and literature. It is, for many of us, the most loved translation. We have memorised its renderings, its cadences work themselves into our prayer and our preaching, and it is, in a unique way our Bible.

For all that, the King James Version is not perfect. No translation is, and, though the seventeenth century translators did their work well, they were not immune from human error, and shared the limitations of their age. But, in addition to these general imperfections, the KJV had two serious limitations built into it by design. Firstly, it was not really a new translation. It was a new translation that Reynolds had called for, and that had been agreed to. Unfortunately, James wanted results quickly, and the amount of time that a completely new translation would take was too great to allow his propagandistic purposes ideally to be served. So, when the translators began their work, their remit had changed. Now they were to concentrate on the revision of existing translations. The situation was made worse by the fact that they were instructed to base their work not on the Geneva translation or on Tyndale, but on the Latinate Bishop's Bible. Happily, the translators knew a good thing when they saw it, and managed to incorporate a great deal of Tyndale into their revision. It has been estimated that the translators of the KJV adopted over eighty percent of Tyndale's renderings.

The second limitation of the KJV also sprang from political considerations. The instructions laid down to guide the translators insisted that they should not alter terms already in ecclesiastical usage. So, for example, while Tyndale had understood that the word *ekklesia* referred neither to a building or a system, and had correctly translated it as 'assembly', the KJV translators rendered it as 'church'. In the first edition of his translation, Tyndale had translated *presbyteros* as 'senior', while the KJV followed the Bishop's Bible in translating the word as 'elder'. Similarly, Tyndale used the word 'love' where the KJV used the more archaic 'charity'. To follow Tyndale in these translations would lend support to the puritan cause, and so scholarship came second to political concerns. In addition to its treatment of ecclesiastical terms, the KJV was a deliberately old-fashioned translation. I Cor. 13 is the outstanding example of this. Where Tyndale used 'love' throughout the chapter, the KJV uses the more dated, and even misleading 'charity'. In general, the KJV is less modern than Tyndale and the Geneva translation even though Tyndale's work had preceded it by more than eighty years.

None of this is intended to deny that the KJV is a very good translation. Indeed, the very fact that it has retained its preeminent position for over four centuries is testament to just how good it is. It could have been even better, but the pressures and politics of the time militated against that. However, the circumstances of its production did prove advantageous in one way.

The work of translating the KJV was carried out by forty-seven of the fifty-four translators that had originally been nominated. These scholars were divided into six committees; two each at Westminster, Oxford, and Cambridge. The members of these committees were chosen solely on the basis of their linguistic ability. So, men like the brilliant Hebraist Lancelot Andrewes, who was, in some ways, almost a Catholic, worked together with puritan scholars like Reynolds and Miles Smith. The presence on the committees of men from all strands within the English church had the advantage of preventing any bias emerging in the translation. Apart from the treatment of ecclesiastical terms enforced on the translators, the KJV is a very impartial translation. It only enhanced that impartiality that the guidelines for the translators also prohibited them from supplying any explanatory notes. In contrast to the voluminous commentary to be found on the pages of the Geneva Bible, the marginalia of the KJV were to be limited to variant readings and cross references. This fact has played no small part in its universal popularity and enduring usefulness.

While we know less about the detail of the process of translating the KJV than we would like, surviving records do provide an insight into the way in which the translators went about their task. We know that the committees were provided with unbound copies of the Bishops Bible, printed on very large sheets. These pages provided the basis from which the translators worked. Each committee was given a particular section of Scripture, and these sections were then divided between the committee members. The individual members worked on their own sections, and their work was reviewed and corrected by the committee as a whole.

The translators' work was completed in 1609 and, two years later, the first editions of the King James Version issued from the presses. The text was revised and corrected in 1769 and, in that version, it has never since been out of print. New editions continue to pour from the printing presses of Bible publishing houses. The KJV is not just the best-selling translation of the Bible ever, but the best-selling book in the history of printing.

The history of Biblical translation is complex. The motives underpinning Biblical translation are likewise complex, especially when we move from the solo projects of devout believers like Tyndale to the sort of committee approach taken by the translators of the KJV and most major modern translations. If this history teaches us nothing else, it confirms for us, time and again, that, behind the sometimes petty and ill-judged considerations that matter to men, the hand of God can be seen at work for the preservation and propagation of His word and the blessing of His people. We have no basis – either historical or theological – for suggesting, as some do, that the translators of the KJV were Divinely inspired in their activity. When we trace its history, however, we receive a compelling reminder of the power and grace of God in taking up flawed human instruments to make mighty and enduring use of them.

CHAPTER 19

The Gathered Church

With the descent of the Holy Spirit on the day of Pentecost, the Church, the body of Christ came into being. This great construction, spanning centuries of time and geographical expanses and including every believer in the Lord Jesus Christ, will continue to be built until the return of Christ and the Rapture signal its perfect completeness. Shortly after this event, another entity came into being. This was the church of God at Jerusalem, the very first local assembly. As the first such gathering, it provides a vital prototype for all that follow. Those 'that gladly received' the message of the Gospel 'were baptized' and 'added unto them' in assembly fellowship Acts 2:41. This company, then, 'continued steadfastly in the apostles' doctrine and fellowship, and in breaking of bread, and in prayers.' As distinct from the global coverage of the church that is the body of Christ, this church was local, confined to Jerusalem. And, as the gospel spread throughout the Roman Empire its progress was marked by the establishment of local assemblies – the churches of God. So, Paul could write to the Corinthians about the necessity to avoid giving offense 'to the Jews, nor to the Gentiles, nor to the church of God' (1 Cor. 10:32). This instruction presupposed a body of individuals marked by their separation and distinctiveness from existing religious and social groupings.

In the early centuries of church testimony this distinctiveness was clearly maintained. In an atmosphere of persecution, where identification with Christ could mean intense suffering, loss, and even death, no one would lightly take the decision to join with the believers. The pattern of conversion, baptism, and joining the local church was the actual, as well as the Scriptural, norm.

In the year 312, this began to change. That year marked the adoption of Christianity by the Roman emperor Constantine. The genuineness or otherwise of Constantine's conversion remains unclear, but its impact on Christendom was undeniably dramatic. Christianity went from being a radical and peripheral religion to become the official religion of the Empire. Once a sure route to persecution and ostracism, Christianity became the pathway to preferment and social advancement. Thus began the identification of church and state that has continued to the present day to the consistent detriment of Scriptural Christianity.

The sphere of Christendom that developed in the centuries after Constantine was very different to the New Testament experience. The acceptance of Christianity by a ruler – whether as the result of conviction or as the fruit of political expediency or dynastic imperatives – was regarded as signalling the wholesale conversion of his people. Baptism, by means of a mistaken analogy with circumcision, lost its Scriptural significance. From being a public act of identification with Christ, entered into by a true believer, it became a meaningless ritual carried out on infants who had no capacity either to believe or reject the gospel.

While there were always those who practiced the scriptural pattern of church testimony, this indiscriminate, national counterfeit became usual. Even the Reformation failed adequately to address this issue. Luther hoped that the German reformation would result in the end of an episcopal hierarchy, and a more obvious working out of the truth of the priesthood of all believers. As a temporary measure Luther approved the transfer of their property and power to Protestant nobles. These nobles were disinclined to relinquish that status, especially in light of the radical and violent events of the Peasant's Revolt. Subsequently, the Peace of Augsburg, which brought the Thirty

Years War to an end, enshrined the principle *cuius regio eius religio* (whose realm, his religion). This meant that the rulers of individual states determined the religion of their state and of their citizens. In England, too, the conversion of the national Church to Protestantism was a purely political decision on the part of Henry VIII and, while his son Edward VI pursued further reformation as a result of his genuine evangelical convictions, membership of the national church remained compulsory for each individual, regardless of their actual views. While the Scottish church differed in that it followed a Presbyterian model, it was still a national church, encompassing everyone – saved or unsaved.

True believers within these national churches realized the difficulty of reconciling this practice with the teaching of Scripture. They attempted to do this by creating the concept of the visible and invisible churches. The visible church, they argued, was the external national church with its ritual and ceremony. The invisible church was made up of true believers, concealed within the visible church, only to be recognized at the Day of Judgement.

However, the period of the Reformation was also marked by the emergence of 'gathered churches'. These groups were made up of those who rejected the joining together of church and state. Such groups had always existed and many, including the Swiss Waldensians and the Czechoslovakian Hussites, gladly identified with the Reformers' teachings on justification by faith alone. Many of these believers insisted that baptism was proper for adults who had been saved and was an essential preliminary for gathering in church capacity. For this reason, they were often identified as 'Anabaptists', meaning 'rebaptisers'. In addition, most Anabaptists maintained the truth of the priesthood of all believers, practised under the control of the Holy Spirit. For this reason, they rejected an ordained ministry, and insisted that believers should have freedom to exercise their spiritual gifts. They were also, for the most part, strongly Biblicist, relying on Scripture, and not church teaching, to guide their lives.

Some Anabaptists held radical and extreme political views, and the influence of these groups led to some horrific events. Anabaptist prophets were, most notably, involved in a notorious siege and massacre at Münster, Germany in 1534. These events hardened public opinion against the Anabaptists, even though many of them were not politically radical. For this reason, 'Anabaptist' was used as a term of reproach, and Anabaptists became the objects of fierce persecution by both Catholics and Protestants throughout Europe. As a result, many fled to the New World, and settled in the colonies of North America.

The Anabaptist movement was concentrated largely in Europe. While some Anabaptists were to be found in England, they were not plentiful. However, similar ideas about the gospel, the church, and baptism were emerging among those who became known as puritans. These believers were dissatisfied with the state of the English church, believing that the Reformation had not gone far enough. As it became increasingly clear that their demands for further reformation would fall upon deaf ears, many puritans became Dissenters – separated from the Church of England. These Dissenters fragmented into a wide variety of groups. Some held very strange doctrines and advocated radical political positions. Most, however, sought the freedom to practice what they understood as the truth of Scripture. Some gathered as congregationalists, some as Presbyterians, and others as Baptists. Each of these groups shared a recognition that only true believers had a place in the visible church, and all sought to separate themselves from the union of Church and state that prevailed in contemporary Christendom.

This was never an easy step to take. Under Elizabeth, James and Charles I, many were persecuted, imprisoned, tortured, and martyred for their obedience to the word of God. After a brief period of prosperity under the rule of Oliver Cromwell, the Restoration brought a fresh wave of oppression. Some escaped to North America, where, in the effective absence of any national church, they found greater freedom to practice their beliefs. They endured faithfully through dark and difficult days, and in the sovereign purposes of God, were to be used mightily by Him in the salvation of countless souls.

Paul reminded the Corinthians that 'God hath chosen the foolish things of the world to confound the wise; and God hath chosen the weak things of the world to confound the things which are mighty' (1:27). In the story of these believers, who took their stand on the word of God, in defiance of the state-sponsored churches with their machinery of compulsion, we can see God using the little things to perform a great work to His glory.

CHAPTER 20

The Evangelical Revival

There is no doubt that studying church history can sometimes be a depressing business. Too often, human frailty and failure seems to hamper or thwart the work of God. But history also has much to encourage us. In particular, it provides us with innumerable proofs of the fact that our sovereign and all-powerful God can overrule human and satanic opposition, and use it to prosper the gospel. The history of the church in the early centuries contains numerous examples of this. Imperial opposition to Christianity, and the consequent scattering of believers, was one of the most effective means of spreading Christianity throughout the known world. Nor are such events confined to the early church. Throughout the centuries, God has used opposition and attack for His purposes and to His ends.

Another example of this principle is provided in the revival of evangelical preaching in the middle of the eighteenth century. In those decades, a mighty work was done for God. In England, Ireland, and America the gospel rang forth with fresh clarity and renewed power. Many individuals were saved, and the character of nations was changed. And this happened not in spite of, but because of the opposition of the established church to the preaching of the gospel.

The Cromwellian interregnum in English history (1649-1660) was marked by a dramatic change in the religious life of the nation. The established Church of England was shaken up, the episcopy or order of bishops was suppressed, and a plethora of independent and separatist congregations sprang up throughout Great Britain and Ireland. The restoration of the monarchy under Charles II brought about a radical reversal. The episcopy was re-established and, in 1662, the Act of Uniformity was passed, requiring ministers to submit to High Church Anglicanism and renounce the puritan and presbyterian elements that had prospered during the Cromwellian period. Over two thousand ministers refused to take the oath to uphold this act and were removed from their positions in an event known as the 'Great Ejection'. Those who continued to preach the gospel became the objects of official persecution – John Bunyan is perhaps the most famous figure to have been imprisoned at this time.

This ejection of those ministers who were most committed to the preaching of the gospel and the practise of Scriptural ecclesiology had a serious and negative impact on the character of the Established Church. This was echoed in fashionable society. The lifting of the social restraints that had been imposed by the puritans resulted in all manner of pleasure seeking. At the same time, the working class continued in spiritual darkness, disregarded by a church that was more concerned with social status than its responsibility to preach the gospel.

It was in this dark context that God began to move. The work that He would accomplish is associated particularly with John and Charles Wesley (1703-1791, 1707-1788) and George Whitefield (1714-1770). These men were instrumental in a great revival of the gospel on both sides of the Atlantic.

John and Charles' father was Samuel Wesley, a clergyman who began his career as a Dissenting minister but who, ironically, is remembered for his opposition to religious non-conformity. Their mother Susanna was a remarkable woman. She gave birth to nineteen children, of which nine died in infancy. She still found time to take charge of her children's education. In addition, she held family devotions every Sunday, and these came to attract a large crowd from the surrounding area who were, like Susanna herself, dissatisfied with the lack of spiritual food provided from the pulpit of the local church. Like many a godly mother, Susanna had a vital impact upon her children. Her exercise to teach her children in her home had international effects that she little imagined.

The Wesley brothers both attended Christ Church, Oxford. While there, they were responsible for founding the 'Holy Club'. This group was made up of young men who were dissatisfied with the low moral standards that prevailed in English society, and sought to live holy lives, marked by religious discipline. This desire made them conspicuous amongst the godless undergraduates, and because of their disciplined lives they became known mockingly as 'Methodists'. Both the Wesley brothers went on to become clergymen. At this stage, though, they were relying on the holiness of their lives for salvation, and knew nothing of the peace of having their sins forgiven. It was only after a disastrous period in the newly established American colony of Georgia, and his return to England that John 'felt [his] heart strangely warmed' as he listened to Luther's preface to Romans being read. In the same month, May 1738, Charles was reading Luther on Galatians, and having found the One 'who loved me and gave himself for me, he was able to say 'I now found myself at peace with God, and rejoice in hope of loving Christ'. Two days later he began writing the first of over six thousand hymns.

George Whitefield was the son of an innkeeper, and went up to Oxford as a servitor, receiving free tuition in exchange for working as a servant for more wealthy students. At Oxford, he too became a member of the 'Holy Club'. In 1735, after a lengthy struggle under the conviction of sin, Whitefield trusted Christ as Saviour. Like the Wesleys, he was ordained and made plans to travel to Georgia. While he waited for his passage, he began to preach in London. He only stayed three months in Georgia, before returning to London. Here he found many pulpits closed to him, by ministers and bishops who had little sympathy with his gospel preaching. It was this effort to stifle the preaching of the gospel that led to the remarkable work of God known as the Evangelical Revival in England and, in America as the first Great Awakening.

Whitefield's response to the closing of pulpits to him was simple but, to the respectable clergymen of the day, almost unthinkable. Shut out of the church in the village of Hanham, near Bristol, Whitefield began to preach in the churchyard. He had been gifted with a remarkably carrying voice, and his sermons quickly gathered enormous crowds, especially of local miners who had never before heard the gospel preached. Soon he was preaching in the open air throughout England. At a time when the population of London was less than 700,000, he attracted audiences of 20,000 to 30,000.

In 1738, Whitefield sailed once more to America. He became parish priest of Savannah, Georgia, where he established the Bethesda orphanage. Before he left, he persuaded the Wesleys to join him in open air preaching. They were reluctant to take this step – John later admitted that he felt it 'almost a sin' to adopt this means. But the brothers were eventually persuaded, and open air preaching became a vital part of the Revival that swept through Britain and the American colonies.

The Wesleys and Whitefield devoted their lives to the preaching of the gospel. Whitefield's greatest work was accomplished in North America, especially in Georgia and Philadelphia. He was associated with Jonathan Edwards, the first great American preacher, who was born in East Windsor, Connecticut in 1703. John itinerated extensively throughout England and Ireland, travelling thousands of miles on horseback, proclaiming the gospel wherever he went. He also organised circuits of preachers, many of whom were not ordained ministers of the Established Church. This led, eventually to the formation of the Methodists. Charles Wesley, likewise, devoted his life to the gospel. He never formally left the Church of England. Though he travelled far less extensively than his brother, his hymns were widely used, and had a profound impact.

The Evangelical Revival has many important lessons for us. It teaches us that social conditions are never so dark as to prevent God working. It demonstrates the inestimable repercussions of a godly mother's exercise. It underscores the value of a disciplined life made wholly available for the Master's service. And it emphasises the power of God to confound His enemies by turning their opposition against themselves.

CHAPTER 21

Rediscovered Hope

Abraham has the distinction, unique in Scripture, of being referred to as the 'friend of God' (James 2:23). This was no empty title, Rather, it reflected the reality of a life lived in communion with God. Seldom was that communion so clearly expressed as when God, anticipating the destruction of Sodom and Gomorrah, revealed his purpose to Abraham, asking 'shall I hide from Abraham that thing which I do?' (Gen 18:17).

Though Abraham's description is unique, his standing is not. It is a remarkable fact that we have, by grace, become friends of God, and that we too have been taken into His confidence. In the upper room, the Lord told His disciples of their new relationship with Himself and with God: 'Henceforth I call you not servants; for the servant knoweth not what his lord doeth: but I have called you friends; for all things that I have heard of my Father I have made known unto you' (Jn 15:15). God's ways are unsearchable, His judgments past finding out. But, in gracious condescension He deigns to open His purposes to our gaze.

Viewed in this context, prophetic Scripture is revealed as one of the chief glories of God's people. It reveals something of His purpose for the Universe, and the ways in which this purpose will be realized. God allows us to live in a present that is enlightened by the future with an ennobling and energizing appreciation of the great goal towards which his purposes ineluctably work.

In light of this, it is both strange and sad that the study of prophecy has, throughout the history of the Church, been relegated to the periphery, discouraged by those in authority and denigrated as the occupation of the mentally – as well as spiritually – unbalanced. The often-quoted quip that the study of Revelation either finds a man mad or leaves him so aptly sums up the prevailing attitude to prophetic study.

It must be acknowledged that history does provide some justification for this attitude. Radical groups throughout the centuries had justified their extreme practices by a reading of prophecy that placed them in the last days. A sorry history of attempts to set the date of Christ's return does little to rehabilitate the caricature of the student of prophecy as at best eccentric, and at worst downright dangerous.

This history helps to explain – though it cannot excuse – the neglect of prophecy. By the end of the fourth century AD, amillennialism had displaced premillennialism as the predominant way of understanding prophecy. Broadly speaking, amillennialists taught that Israel had been replaced by the Church, which enjoys a spiritual fulfilment of the promises originally given to Israel. They denied the possibility of a literal millennium, arguing instead that Christendom was already experiencing a spiritual millennium. The Reformers generally accepted the outlines of the amillennial scheme, and, in the aftermath of violent social upheaval caused by millennial teaching, vigorously opposed the idea of a literal thousand-year reign of Christ.

Throughout the seventeenth century though, this began to change. The resistance to allegorical readings of Scripture, which was at the heart of the Reformation, resulted in a grammatical-historical interpretation that insisted that the Bible meant what it said. This made a spiritualised amillennial reading difficult to sustain. These were also times of remarkable progress in almost every field of human endeavour. The world seemed to be becoming a better place. This spirit of optimism was reflected theologically in postmillennialism. This view suggests that the spread of the gospel, with its beneficial effects on all levels of human society, would usher in an idyllic period of a thousand years at the end of which Christ would return. Postmillennialism depicted human history and contemporary society in a positive light. It became widely held among evangelicals, and may well have helped to foster their enthusiasm for spreading the gospel at home and abroad.

At the end of the eighteenth century, though, this optimism was becoming difficult to sustain. Progress in scientific discovery seemed to be leading man away from, and not towards God; atheistic rationalism blossomed and revolutions in France, Ireland, and America seemed to prefigure a wider descent into social anarchy. These circumstances encouraged believers to look again at Scripture, and to return to the premillennialism that had been little-regarded since the early centuries of the Church. Premillennialists expected that 'evil men and seducers' would, indeed, 'wax worse and worse' (2 Tim 3:13). Society was on a downward slope and its decline would only be arrested and reversed by the return of Christ, Who would put down rebellion and establish His righteous kingdom.

In this context, a variety of premillennialism interpretations emerged. Most students of prophecy adopted an historicist premillennialism, which understood the book of Revelation to refer to past events. The crucial insight that it referred to future events we owe to John Nelson Darby (1800-1882).

Darby was born into a wealthy Irish family. He was an extraordinary man with a forceful personality and seemingly inexhaustible energy. Although his father intended him to be a lawyer, Darby chose to become a clergyman in the established Church of Ireland, ministering to poor parishioners in Co. Wicklow. He adopted an ascetic lifestyle and, by his own admission was a high churchman, who thought that salvation was only to be found within the established episcopal church.

This changed in 1827 when Darby, immobilized by a serious riding accident, devoted his convalescence to the study of

Scripture. His conversion, which he described as his 'deliverance from bondage' can be traced to this period. While his understanding of prophecy (and his views on the nature of the church, which fall outside the scope of this chapter) developed over time, it is probable that it, too, had its roots in this time of meditation and Bible study.

Darby's interpretation of prophecy had a number of important features. Like many evangelicals of the time, Darby was convinced that God still had a purpose for Israel, and that the promises made to the nation would yet be fulfilled. This led him to endorse a strongly literal understanding of Scripture that insisted that the term 'Israel' always referred to the nation, and never meant the Church. This principle also meant that he understood the book of Revelation to be a literal account of evens that were still to take place and not a coded account of the history of the Church. (This view is usually called futurist premillennialism.)

Like many other earlier scholars, Darby identified a number of distinct periods in human history, marked by the different ways in which God dealt with man. These 'dispensations' were far from being the most distinctive element of Darby's system, but they gave it the name – dispensationalism – by which it is most commonly known.

The most distinctive feature of Darby's interpretation was related to Christ's return. Other Premillennialists at the time saw this as a single event in which Christ returned to Earth, after the Tribulation, to establish His kingdom. As Darby studied the New Testament, he came to realize that it presents the return of Christ as an event in two stages. First is the Rapture, when He comes to the air to snatch away the saints, living and dead. This event is followed by the seven years of the Tribulation, at the end of which Christ returns to Earth in glory and with His saints to rule in righteousness for a thousand glorious years.

After his conversion Darby's life was devoted to preaching

and teaching. He travelled widely, crisscrossing the Atlantic and working extensively in Europe. He produced a new English translation of the Bible, and oversaw the translation of the Bible into German and French. He was an indefatigable writer, producing over 40 volumes of commentary, controversy, and exhortation, as well as some of the most sublime hymns ever written. This activity meant that dispensationalism was accepted by many Christians, especially in the United States, where the Bible Conference movement and the publication, in 1907, of *The Scofield Reference Bible* did much to ensure its spread.

We have much cause to thank God for the ministry of J.N. Darby. His saturation in Scripture resulted in his being used to recover the Church's delight in prophecy and to restore her expectation of the imminent return of the Lord Jesus. For Darby, and for generations of believers since, that hope has glowed brightly, even as conditions round about have grown increasingly gloomy. May we, too, be found among those who 'love His appearing'(2 Tim. 4:8).

Maranatha, even so come, Lord Jesus!

CHAPTER 22

The Recovery of Church Truth

A local church, as envisaged by Scripture, is a remarkable entity. It exists as a called-out company of believers gathered in the name of the Lord Jesus Christ (Matt. 18:20). It is part of no overarching organisation, but stands on its own, observed by and directly responsible to its risen Lord (Rev. 1-3). Those who form part of it have first been saved, and then have publically acknowledged that faith in baptism. The church is led by a plurality of elders (Acts 14:23, Acts 20:17), who are also described as shepherds (1 Tim. 3:1-2, Tit. 1:7) and overseers (the meaning of the word translated as 'bishop' in the King James Version) (Acts 20:28). Its activities include the 'breaking of bread', prayer, the teaching of God's word, the spread of the gospel, and ministering to the material needs of individual saints and other churches (Acts 2: 42, 1 Thes. 2:18, 2 Cor. 8:2, Philip. 4:10). It is striking that so simple an entity, without elaborate governance, ornate premises, or the support of a great organisation, should be described as the 'temple of God'. Yet, it is this sort of company that Scripture describes as the 'church of God', and it knows of no other place where Christ's blood-bought people can gather in His name and with His presence.

Wherever the apostles witnessed, these churches were the result. Sadly, though, even before the apostolic period had come to an end, there was evidence of a shift away from the simplicity of the Scriptural pattern. Men like Diotrephes arose, loving to have pre-eminence amongst God's people (3 Jn 1:9). In the early centuries following the death of the apostles, the influence of such men increased. A scriptural plurality of elders was replaced by a single ruling elder, and local responsibility gave way to federated central authority. Thus, the scriptural understanding of the church as a local spiritual entity was displaced by a supranational church, which wielded enormous political – and indirectly military – power, and that placed unsaved and venal men in authority over God's people.

It is easy, as we read the history of this institutional church and the other national churches that emerged from it, to assume that this authority was total and inescapable. In reality, however, there were always those, in all parts of the world, who gathered in Scriptural simplicity. Often the subject of persecution, and with little incentive to advertise their existence, they have left little trace on the pages of history. It is important not to forget about these faithful believers. The recovery of truth about the nature of the church that took place in the early decades of the nineteenth century was unusual in the breadth and longevity of its results, but in its return to the teaching of the New Testament it shared much with other movements that had gone to the same source. To understand this historical context is not to underestimate or devalue the remarkable work that was accomplished by the Holy Spirit, but it may preserve us from arrogance or complacency about our place in Divine purpose.

Inevitably, though, the events that took place in Dublin in the late 1820s must have a special interest for any believer in assembly fellowship. It was there that a small group of believers began to gather, in separation from the surrounding denominations, and in obedience to the simplicity of the Scriptural pattern.

These believers had ample reason to be dissatisfied with the state of the Established Church. The Anglican Church of Ireland was at a low spiritual ebb. Many of its ministers saw their calling as merely a source of employment, and the interests of the gospel and the souls of the perishing came a poor second to maintaining the social status and political power of the church. Those ministers who too plainly preached the gospel were liable to be silenced by their bishop. In the last half of the eighteenth century, a number of these ministers had seceded from the Church, impatient to preach the gospel without hindrance. Some had established their own preaching networks or denominations, most notably the Walkerites and the Kellyites. These denominations had little doctrinal basis, beyond their evangelical imperative and in light of this it is not surprising that they had limited impact, and were only short-lived.

By contrast, the believers who began to meet together in Dublin in the 1820s had no interest in forming themselves into another denomination. Though they included men of great intellectual ability, high social position and considerable personal charisma, they did not gather to or under any of these. Instead, they gathered to the name of Christ, in distinction to the denominations around them. Their convictions about the church, and the way in which believers were to gather owed little to centuries of church tradition, and much to their saturation in Scripture. The place that they gave to God's word is reflected in their love of conversational Bible readings, and this form of teaching has remained a distinctive feature of many assemblies.

The willingness of these men to be guided by Scripture alone meant that their gatherings looked very different from the prevailing practice of Christendom. The Reformation had recovered the Biblical truth of the priesthood of all believers in theory, but it continued to be denied in practice. Those who gathered in Dublin believed that the office of the clergyman was, in J.N. Darby's words, 'a sin against the Holy Ghost', and they allowed for the exercise of gift by all brethren who possessed it.

Some of those who gathered in Dublin lived in, or had strong ties with England, and the principles expressed in the gatherings in Dublin soon crossed the Irish Sea. One of the first assemblies in Great Britain was in Plymouth. Those who gathered refused to adopt any unscriptural name. This frustrated those who wanted to label this new movement, and, focusing on the characteristic mode of address amongst these believers and their location, they gave them the name 'Plymouth Brethren'. (Had they called them 'Dublin Brethren, it would have been more historically accurate, though just as unscriptural.)

The teaching of these brethren found open ears and hearts in many places. The speed with which this teaching spread indicated that the Spirit of God was at work, preparing the hearts of God's people and directing and empowering the work of revival. He was at work, too, continuing to lead His people into truth. So, as the decades passed, a clearer understanding emerged of the distinctiveness of the local assembly, and the need for separation from the religious confusion of Christendom. Progress was not uninterrupted – opposition from without and division within did their best to strangle the work of God. But, in spite of these challenges, God's work carried on, and assemblies were formed throughout the world.

The evangelical zeal of believers in assemblies had no small part to play in this progress. At home and on the mission field, these believers were active in the spread of the gospel. In gospel halls, tents and in the open-air they laboured to discharge their responsibility to their fellow men. Missionaries commended by assemblies in the United Kingdom and Ireland were responsible for pioneering in China, in Central Africa, in India, and in South America. They eschewed the support of missionary societies, and relied on God to supply their needs. These devoted servants of God echoed something of the energy and devotion of the apostles and, like them, 'turned the world upside down.'

The history of the assemblies over the past century has not always been a positive story. At all times, though, it is an important one. Time and again, the experience of God's people has proved that strength in testimony directly depends on obedience to God's word, and separation from the world – socially, religiously and politically. When the principles of Scripture are compromised, decline and decay are inevitable. Too often, truth that was hard-bought by earlier generations has been frittered away by those who undervalued or despised their birthright and inheritance.

We live in a dramatically different world from the Dublin of the 1820s. It is even more different from the world inhabited by the believers of the first century. But God's pattern for His people has not changed, and we understand very little about God if we doubt that His pattern is best.

CHAPTER 23

Evaluating a Translation

This book has attempted, among other things, to describe how it was that we got our Bible. To answer this question, we have looked at the ancient origins of Scripture, at the way in which God safeguarded the survival of His Word, and the ways in which men of God dedicated their lives to the task of translating Scripture into the English vernacular. We have come to 1611 and the translation of the King James Version.

This may seem a strange point to stop. Four centuries have passed since the KJV first appeared, and it is certainly not the case that the intervening years have been barren of translation. In fact, it has been estimated that at least three thousand translations of Scripture into English have appeared since 1611. Some of these versions have been noteworthy, many have been helpful, and some, sadly, have been perversions of God's word and its truth. All, however, lie outside the direct scope of this book. There are a number of reasons for this. This volume has sought to tell the story of how we got our Bible and this is, perhaps, a description better fitted by the KJV than by any other translation. Furthermore, while the histories of many later translations are of interest to the specialist, they are far more prosaic affairs than those that have occupied us so far. And, of course, one has to stop somewhere.

Before concluding, however, it is worth our while to extend the scope of our discussion by thinking about how we evaluate a translation of Scripture. Not all translations are equally good and, given the importance that we do and should attach to the Word of God, it is vital that we think carefully about our choice of translation. This is particularly true when we think of our main translation. Most of us, in our private reading and Bible study, will refer to a range of versions – this is a very valuable practice, and can often give us a clearer understanding of the truth of Scripture. However, using a translation in this supplementary way is a different thing from selecting the main translation for our individual and collective use. When it is this decision that we are making, a number of important factors need to be carefully considered.

Textual Base

Every effort to provide a translation of the Bible has to begin by making a fundamental decision about the manuscripts that are to be used as a basis for that translation. This is not a simple decision. As Scripture was copied through the centuries, a number of variants were introduced. Sometimes these were introduced inadvertently, by copyists' errors, and sometimes deliberately, by scribes who expanded or amplified passages, in an effort to make their meaning clearer. Textual critics are scholars who study the transmission of these manuscripts. They attempt to identify, categorise, and account for these variants. By looking at the variant readings that are common to different manuscripts, these scholars identify a number of textual families. Manuscripts within each family share a common history.

Most scholars identify four such families: the Alexandrine, Byzantine, Caesarean, and the Western. Of these, the Alexandrine and the Byzantine are the most important. Only a very small group of manuscripts in the Alexandrine family survive. They all originate in North Africa, and they include some of the oldest surviving manuscripts of Scripture. The *Codex Sinaiticus*, which was discovered in the library of the Monastery of Saint Catherine, Mount Sinai in the middle of the nineteenth century, and the *Codex Vaticanus* are the two most famous examples of this text type. The Byzantine family comprises by far the largest number of surviving manuscripts, but those that survive are later in their date than those of the Alexandrine type. After about the fourth century AD, the Byzantine text type became the standard followed in both Eastern and Western Christendom. It was the version used in the Greek-speaking Byzantine Empire, and it underpinned Erasmus's Novum Testamentum, and all of the significant European translations of the Reformation period. Erasmus' text became known as the Textus Receptus, or the received text, after the term was used in the preface to the 1633 edition of his work.

Manuscripts within each of these text types are not identical with each other. However, the differences between two Alexandrine manuscripts tend to be significantly fewer than the differences between an Alexandrine and a Byzantine text would be. It is important to stress that even these differences are minor, and none have a definitive bearing on any doctrine of Christianity.

When the translators of the King James Version undertook their work, very few manuscripts of the Alexandrine text-type had been discovered. Because of this, and because their work was so closely tied to the earlier English translations, their translation was firmly based on the Byzantine text-type. With the exception of the New King James version, which preserves the textual basis of the King James, most modern translations use an eclectic textual base. Translators look at the variants across the manuscript families, and decide which readings are more likely to be correct. Usually, the oldest reading is the one preferred and so, in practice, the Alexandrine text-type tends to take priority in most modern translations.

Choosing a preferred translation of Scripture, therefore, also involves making a choice about a preferred textual base. This is a very complex question, but essentially it boils down to a question of whether an older reading is more likely to be correct, or whether a more widely attested reading should be preferred. The preponderance of modern scholarship comes down on the side of the oldest reading, but there are weighty and convincing arguments in favour of accepting a reading that had more widespread support.

Those who are interested in looking at this subject in detail will find some recommendations for further reading in the last chapter of this book. However, it is vital to stress that, though this debate is important, the textual – as opposed to translational – differences between different versions of the Bible are slight, and do not introduce any lack of clarity or ambiguity to any doctrine.

Principles of Translation

There are essentially two approaches that are adopted to Biblical translation. One, often called formal or literal equivalence or essentially literal translation, attempts, as far as possible, to convey the meaning of the original word-for-word. These translations are the most faithful. However, because of the differences in word-order and other features of the language, they can seem wooden in their style at times. The other method of translation, usually called dynamic equivalence is less wedded to the words of the text, and translates thought-for-thought. These versions prioritise easy readability and, in theory at least, good style, above faithfully reproducing the literal content of Scripture. Dynamic equivalence requires the translator to identify the thought that is being communicated, and translation and interpretation become dangerously entangled. For the believer in the verbal inspiration of Scripture, this is not a difficult choice to make. We seek 'the words of eternal life', not the general thoughts. John Nelson Darby, a translator of considerable ability and experience, who oversaw the translation of the Bible into English, German, and French clearly stated the issue in question in the preface to his German translation:

> We might indeed have clothed many passages in more elegant German, but, without being in bondage to words, we have been governed throughout by the thought that the faithful rendering of the original text outweighs every other consideration; and the more so because we believe with the very fullest conviction the divine inspiration of the holy scriptures as the

revelation of the infinite wisdom of God, and the expression of His gracious character in Jesus Christ. But since no one is able to grasp the whole expanse of this revelation, and often a meaning beyond the comprehension of the translator lies hidden in a sentence, which would be lost in a free translation but may be found in a more literal one, through deeper teaching of the Holy Spirit — it is evidently necessary to reproduce the original text as in a mirror. (*Collected Works*, 13: 168)

It must be acknowledged that no translation is totally formally equivalent, but we should ensure that we use one that is as close as possible. In today's Bible marketplace this limits our choice considerably. As belief in the verbal inspiration of Scripture has weakened in Christendom, the trend in modern translations has been away from formal equivalence. The KJV, the Revised Version, the New King James Version, the New American Standard Bible, and the English Standard Version are all regarded as essentially literal translations. However, only the KJV and the NASB take literal equivalence seriously enough to identify additional words supplied by the translators to help the sense by setting them in italics. For the reader who is committed to the plenary verbal inspiration of Scripture, this is an essential feature. The commitment of the KJV translators to the word-for-word meaning of the text is one of the major advantages of this translation.

English Style

On the face of it, this might seem a frivolous consideration when choosing a translation: it is not. It was once fashionable to argue, as C.S. Lewis most notably did, that Scripture ought to be translated in as ordinary a style as possible. Those who took this view point, quite correctly, to the fact that the *koine* Greek of the New Testament is not the language of literary or rhetorical endeavour, but the everyday language of the common people. What they fail to take account of, however, is that the writers of the New Testament use this language, with great effect, vividly to convey a variety of styles from the simple narrative of Mark's gospel to the close legal reasoning of Paul's epistles, and the visionary language of Revelation. The Old Testament manifests, if anything, an even greater array of literary styles. The transmission of this is one of the greatest weaknesses of most modern translations. Though some of them have included in their translating committees specialists in English, they seem either to have chosen these specialists poorly, or to have ignored their advice. The variety and verve of Scripture are flattened into a dull mediocrity. This cannot but impoverish our public gatherings. Scripture need not be couched in complicated and out-dated language. But the version of the Bible that gives texture to our worship, our prayer, and our preaching ought to have a dignity of language, and a versatility of style that do justice to the original.

Preference as to style is inevitably a subjective matter. However, it is difficult to think of any modern translation that matches the majesty of the KJV. Translated as the English language enjoyed its heyday of literary achievement, it was translated by men whose other writings clearly indicate that they did not need the advice of 'style consultants'. These men were united in their appreciation of the importance of God's word, and they did their best to ensure that it was expressed in the best that English had to offer. In doing so, they helped to shape that language, and their translation is hard to beat for beauty and, on the whole and certain archaisms notwithstanding, for clarity.

The stylistic advantages of the KJV become particularly clear when we think about memorising Scripture. Memorising Scripture in some modern translations is about as easy as learning off an instruction manual. The cadences and rhythms of the KJV commend themselves to the memory as well as to the ear, and assist us in the invaluable exercise of memorising the word of God.

Collective Practice

When we are choosing our main translation of Scripture, it is very important to bear in mind the translation that is used in the assembly of which we form part. The confusion caused by the use of multiple versions in the public reading or quotation of Scripture is best avoided. And, as we will find the words of the translation that we most use in private reading and Bible study coming most readily to mind, it makes sense to be guided in our individual choice by collective practice. This, it must be stressed again, does not mean that we cannot or should not consult other translations. It does mean that we ought carefully to consider the benefit of the assembly and of all those who attend our meetings in our choice of translation.

CHAPTER 24

Conclusion and Recommended Reading

In the eleventh chapter of the epistle to the Hebrews the writer details an impressive list of the heroes of faith. These worthies, named and unnamed, throughout history are singled out as exemplars of the life of faith. The list makes for stirring, if humbling, reading.

And it is the writer's intention to stir us. In 12:1 he highlights the practical implications of the example of 'so great a cloud of witnesses' for the way in which we live our lives. But he also takes pains to ensure that we give the examples of the past a proper place in our thought, as he exhorts us to look off 'unto Jesus, the author and finisher of faith'.

That priority is worth restating as we come to the close of this volume. As we have looked back – in a necessarily compressed and superficial way – over the centuries of church testimony, we have seen much to challenge and stir us. In the words of Longfellow,

> Lives of great men all remind us
> We can make our lives sublime.
> And, departing, leave behind us
> Footprints in the sands of time.

But these chapters will have failed in their purpose if they have not emphasized for us the necessity to look off beyond man, to look to God and His word as the only sufficient and reliable guide for our life and testimony. History holds many valuable lessons for us, but we should be careful to keep it in its place. Especially should we be very cautious about appealing to historical precedent to justify doctrine or practice. Whether we appeal to the 'early Fathers' or to the 'early Brethren', we are alike on uncertain ground. 'What saith the Scriptures?' (Rom. 4:3) must be our inveterate question; God's word must be our first, our last, our only court of appeal.

It is also important that our consideration of history should enhance, and not hamper, our activity in the present. It is easy to allow a preoccupation with the past – recent or distant – to paralyze us. The apostle Paul, in his personal experience, found it necessary to forget that which was behind, in order that he might 'press forward.' We should not forget history, but we should seek to maintain the attitude outlined by Dan Crawford, the idiosyncratic African missionary: 'hats off to the past, coats off to the future.'

These considerations notwithstanding, we do have much to learn from history, and a people that forgets its past is impoverished indeed. To trace the faithfulness of God, and the power of His Word should fit us better for worship and for work.

These chapters have provided an overview of some important themes and moments in church history. They have drawn on some of the sources mentioned below, and they are a useful place from which to embark on a more detailed study. Providing lists of this sort is always a slightly risky exercise, and it should be stated that the inclusion of a book is not an endorsement of every detail of its content. Writing history requires two components – facts and interpretation. We can value a work for its presentation of fact, even while disagreeing – wholly or in part – with the author's interpretation of those facts. Indeed, it is healthy to have our own views challenged from time to time.

Covering two millennia in a work of reasonable size is difficult. Nonetheless, there are a number of useful overviews of church history. Iain D. Campbell's *Heroes and Heretics* devotes one brief chapter to each century, and provides a readable, though sketchy account. Also useful is E.H. Broadbent's classic work *The Pilgrim Church*. Broadbent attempts to tell the story of the non-institutional church, of companies of believers who were often subject to severe persecution by the Roman Catholic church, and by the national churches of the Reformation. His accounts often differ markedly from the received view of the groups that he describes. It is unfortunate, therefore, that editions currently available do not provide adequate documentation of the sources used. In spite of this, *The Pilgrim Church* is fascinating reading, and a valuable reminder that there are at least two sides to every story.

More detailed coverage of the early centuries of church history is provided by F.F. Bruce's *The Spreading Flame*. The story of Christianity from the apostolic period through to the Reformation is told with admirable clarity by Nick R. Needham in his three volume work, *2000 Years of Christ's Power*. Each volume stands on its own, and they are especially useful for their inclusion of relevant primary sources at the end of each chapter. Volume 3, *Renaissance and Reformation* is especially useful, and covers not only the magisterial Reformation, but also the story of the Anabaptists. The opening chapters of David Bebbington's *Baptists through the Centuries* are also useful in this context, especially for their summary of the debate about the scale of Anabaptist influence on English nonconformity.

While our chapters have looked back to the origins of Scripture and traced their path through Greek and Latin, we have concentrated especially on the Bible in English. Obviously, this is only a part of the story. An excellent overview of the wider history of the transmission and translation of Scripture can be found in Christopher De Hamel's *The Book: A History of the Bible*. This book is particularly valuable for its illustrations – it provides beautiful photographs of some of the most important versions of Scripture. For the story of the English Bible, David Daniell's *The Bible in English: History and Influence* is essential reading. At precisely 900 pages long it is not a small book, but it is both comprehensive and outstandingly readable. Daniell begins with the earliest manuscript versions in English, and closes by discussing the twentieth-century translations. *En route* he discusses a fascinating range of material. His work is deeply scholarly and highly enjoyable. F.F. Bruce's *History of the Bible in English* covers the same ground, more briefly and, it must be said, less entertainingly, than Daniell. At a more popular level, Ken Connolly's *The Indestructible Book* is a much briefer account of the history of the English Bible. At a more scholarly level, Alfred Pollard's *Records of the English Bible: The Documents relating to the Translation and Publication of the Bible in English, 1525-1611* is a very valuable collection. Originally published in 1911, it has recently been made available in an affordable modern printing.

At the beginning of this book, we looked at the inspiration and transmission of Scripture in Greek and Latin. *The Text of the New Testament* by Bruce M. Metzger provides, in its earlier chapters, an excellent discussion of the production and transmission of the earliest copies of Scripture. Its later chapters, which discuss textual criticism provide a clear account of the history and practice of the discipline. Some of the widely-accepted conclusions of textual criticism have been challenged by Eta Linnemann in *Biblical Criticism on Trial.* Her argument is complex, and heavily statistical and not, perhaps, for the faint of heart. A shorter and more accessible discussion is provided in Malcolm Watt's *The Lord Gave the Word: A Study in the History of the Biblical Text.* Also valuable are F.F. Bruce's *The New Testament Documents: Are they Reliable?* and *The Books and the Parchments.* The latter book provides an especially useful discussion of the formation of the Old Testament and New Testament canons.

The name of William Tyndale must loom large in any account of the history of the English Bible. The story of his life makes fascinating reading, and numerous writers have essayed their version. The definitive biography, though, is David Daniell's *William Tyndale: A Biography.* As with *The Bible in English,* this book demonstrates Daniell's ability to couch scholarly discussion in clear, readable, and often humorous prose. His deep admiration for Tyndale is clear, and gives this book a warmth and charm unusual in scholarly biographies. We also have Daniell to thank for his editions of Tyndale's writings, including his translations of the Old and New Testaments. These are not merely historical oddities – to read Tyndale's translation is to be struck by the magnitude of his achievement as a translator of Scripture.

The Geneva Bible has been strangely neglected by scholars and, while it has recently been the object of increased study, there is still a lack of material on its translation and influence. However, note should be taken of *The Geneva Bible: A Facsimile of the 1560 Edition*, recently published by Hendrickson. This is of interest both for the quality of the translation and for the additional material provided. In addition to the famous – or infamous – marginalia, this edition of the Geneva Bible is illustrated by detailed woodcuts. Those depicting the construction and furnishings of the tabernacle are still not without value.

As we have seen, the King James Version of the Bible is of enormous importance in the history of the English Bible. Oddly enough, given the status it was to achieve, the poor record-keeping of the translators means that we have only a partial insight into the history of its translation. A useful primary source is Miles Smith's preface 'The Translators to the Reader'. This is omitted from most modern printings of the KJV, but is available on-line. Two reliable popular accounts of the translation of the KJV are available: Alistair McGrath's *In the Beginning: The Story of the King James Bible and How It Changed a Nation, a Language, and a Culture* and Adam Nicholson's *Power and Glory: Jacobean England and the making of the King James Bible* (published in the USA as *God's Secretaries: The Making of the King James Bible*). Gordon Campbell's *Bible: The Story of the King James Version, 1611-2011* is also a useful source of information.

David Bebbington's *Evangelicalism in Modern Britain* is the standard introduction to the emergence and growth of the evangelical movement in Britain. That subject can also be approached by way of biographies of the main figures involved, and John Pollock's biographies of John Wesley, George Whitefield, William Wilberforce, and D.L. Moody are readable and stimulating, and do an excellent job of filling in the American context.

The stories of the recovery of dispensational truth, and the truth of gathering in assembly capacity are closely intertwined. Timothy Stunt's *From Awakening to Secession* is a meticulously detailed account that describes the background to these events in some detail, and provides unparalleled coverage of the ministry of Darby and others in Ireland, the UK, and on the continent. Grayson Carter's *Evangelical Secessions from the Via Media, c.1800-1850* is also useful in this context. In light of John Nelson Darby's importance to both these stories, it is worth consulting Max Weremchuk's *John Nelson Darby: A Biography* and, in a less scholarly vein, Marion Field's *John Nelson Darby: Prophetic Pioneer.* For all his importance, Darby was only one of God's servants, and the stories of two other giants are told in Edwin Cross's *The Irish Saint and Scholar – A biography of William Kelly* and his *Life and Times of C.H. Mackintosh.* The influence of C.I. Scofield's Reference Bible, and the way in which it was used to spread dispensational truth are discussed in Todd Mangum and Mark S. Sweetnam, *The Scofield Reference Bible.*

The early story of those believers who are identified – often against their wishes – as 'the Brethren' is told in David J. Beattie, *The Brethren: the Story of a Great Recovery* and in Harold H. Rowden's *The Origins of the Brethren 1825-1850.*

These are just a handful of the countless volumes available to assist us in tracing the history of God's dealings with His church. That history contains much to sadden. Human failure is writ large in every age of history – not least in our own. But history has its greatest value for us when it reminds us of the faithfulness of God, His power to preserve testimony and the provision that He has made for the unique needs of every generation in His holy word.

It is the author's prayer that the story told in this volume will have the effect of sending the reader back, with increased appreciation, to The Book of Books. As we appreciate something of the infinite grace of God in speaking to humanity, and of His wisdom and providence in inspiring and preserving the text of Holy Scripture we must, of necessity, value more highly the content of that revelation. And, as we recall with gratitude the dedicated scholarship and devoted sacrifices of the godly men who gave themselves to the cause of bringing the light of Divine revelation to successive generations, may God give us help to profit by their example, to match their commitment to the Word of God and its truth. In the words of John Purvey, 'God grant to us all grace to know well and to keep well holy writ, and to suffer joyfully some pain for it at the last.'

> *Wherefore seeing we also are compassed about with so great a cloud of witnesses, let us lay aside every weight, and the sin which doth so easily beset us, and let us run with patience the race that is set before us, Looking unto Jesus the author and finisher of our faith; who for the joy that was set before him endured the cross, despising the shame, and is set down at the right hand of the throne of God.*

Hebrews 12:1-2